# PLAYS
# FOR
# PLEASURE

# PLAYS FOR PLEASURE

**Edited by
Sadler and Hayllar**

Illustrated by Bruce Baldwin

M

First published 1984 by
THE MACMILLAN COMPANY OF AUSTRALIA PTY LTD
107 Moray Street, South Melbourne 3205
6 Clarke Street, Crows Nest 2065
Reprinted 1985, 1986, 1987 (twice)

Associated companies and representatives
throughout the world

National Library of Australia
cataloguing in publication data

Sadler, R. K. (Rex Kevin).
    Plays for pleasure.

    For secondary school students.
    ISBN 0 333 38083 5.

    1. College and school drama.  I. Hayllar, T. A. S.
    (Thomas Albert S.).  II. Title.

A822′.3

Set in Baskerville and Helios by Setrite Typesetters, Hong Kong
Printed in Hong Kong

# Contents

# Acknowledgements

The editors and publishers are grateful to the following for permission to reproduce copyright material.

Allan Mackay for *The Fortress* and *A Taste of Wine*; Greg Shepherd for *A Star Is Spawn*; Bill Tordoff and David Doughan, and Heinemann Educational (Drama Department), for *Ticket to Hitsville*; Dorrington Publications for *The Ghost of Muddledump Manor!*; Maureen Stewart for *Snow Bright and the Seven Wharfies*; Bill Condon and Dianne Bates for *Numbers at the Gate*; Samuel French Ltd for *Hiss the Villain!*; Spike Milligan for *The Affair of the Lone Banana*.

*The Canterville Ghost* may be performed without permission or payment of a fee in school-related activities, provided acknowledgement is made to the playwright.

The following plays may not be performed without the permission of their copyright owners, as specified:

*The Fortress* and *A Taste of Wine* — Allan Mackay, Rose Valley Road, Gerringong, NSW 2534.

*Ticket to Hitsville* — Heinemann Educational (Drama Department), The Press at Kingswood, Tadworth, Surrey, UK.

*A Star Is Spawn* — Greg Shepherd, c/– Westbourne Grammar School, Sayers Road, Werribee, Vic. 3030.

*The Ghost of Muddledump Manor!* — Alan Rowe, c/– Dorrington Publications, 4 Shirley Avenue, Glen Waverley, Vic. 3150.

*Numbers at the Gate* — Dianne Bates, 86 Bridge Street, Coniston, NSW 2500.

*The Affair of the Lone Banana* — Spike Milligan, c/– Norma Farnes, 9 Orme Court, London W2, UK.

*Hiss the Villain!* — Samuel French Ltd, 26 Southampton Street, The Strand, London WC2E 7JE, UK.

Enquires regarding performance or reproduction of *Snow Bright and the Seven Wharfies* should be addressed to The Macmillan Company of Australia, 107 Moray Street, South Melbourne, Vic. 3205.

# Preface

In this selection we have assembled ten more plays that we believe 'work' in the classroom, can be performed on stage without elaborate props, and, above all, provide students with plenty of enjoyment. They are all plays for pleasure — the pleasure of humorous *or* dramatic role-playing, of the unusual or far-fetched, of the madcap or slick, of the imaginative....

The plays in this book are successful in the classroom because they offer what students have a right to expect in any play: entertainment. Our aim, as always, is instruction through enjoyment. Following each play are questions relating to comprehension, interpretation and response; they can act as effective starting-points for class discussion.

# A Star is Spawn.

Greg Shepherd

## Cast

King Jerome
Wizard
Royal Advisor (Milton)
Royal Accountant
Lackey
Prince Egbert
Princess Prudence
Witch (Lucrezia)
Trixie
Prince Slobov
Peasant Spokesman
Peasant Ringleader
Peasant 1
Peasant 2
Messenger
Narrator

## SCENE 1

*The court of King Jerome of Lower Slobovnia. The **Narrator** stands at the front of the stage, a little to one side. In the background we see a dejected **King Jerome** frozen in meditation sitting on the throne. To the left of the throne stands the **Royal Advisor** and a little further to the left of him stands the **Wizard**. The background scene is painted in a manner reminiscent of a medieval castle. On the extreme right of the stage the **Lackey** stands stiffly to attention. When the **Narrator** begins his speech the other characters remain completely motionless.*

**Narrator**   Let us imagine a time long ago on a continent far away in an age long before man had flown to the moon or dreamed up such wonderful inventions as the pop-up toaster or the hot-water bottle. On this imaginary continent let us further imagine two kingdoms with the unlikely-sounding names Upper Slobovnia and Lower Slobovnia. At the time in which our play is set Upper Slobovnia had waged war against Lower Slobovnia for many a long day. For years King Jerome had looked for a way of ending the war without loss of face (or any other part of the body for that matter). You see, Upper Slobovnia was a happy and contented realm ruled strictly but fairly by the balding King Walter. Not so for Lower Slobovnia. For years strikes, unemployment and famine plagued the Lower Kingdom. Then things really started to go downhill. The King of Lower Slobovnia was in Dire Straits. Eventually, however, he had to end his holiday in Dire Straits and come home and try and solve some of the kingdom's problems.

King Jerome had a son who, curiously enough, was a prince. He also had a daughter who, by another remarkable coincidence, happened to be a princess. He had dreamed for a long time of the possibility that either his son or his daughter might marry into King Walter's family and so end hostilities between the two nations. But alas, it seemed that this was not to be. His daughter, Princess Prudence, had been laid up in bed since the age of four, when she had taken ill after swallowing the fish-bone of a mullet. And Prince Egbert would never consent to a love match because he was a true child of nature; better content chasing butterflies, talking to flowers or lying idly on the bank

KING JEROME

of a pond in the woods than in the passionate embrace of a lady from abroad. He was not one for foreign affairs.

Our play begins with the King in heated discussion with his ministers.

(*Characters in the background now come to life as the spotlight on the* **Narrator** *fades and the stage lights come up.*)

**Advisor**  But sire, the peasants have no bread. They are starving to death. Disease and famine are on the doorstep of nearly every household in the country.

**King**  Stop trying to humour me, Milton, and get on with the bad news.

**Advisor**  The kingdom of Lower Slobovnia is tottering on the brink of collapse.

**King**  Never mind that. Is my pinstripe suit back from the dry-cleaners yet?

**Advisor**  But sire, it is not a thing to make light of. (*in a hushed voice*) And, noble sire, I have heard tell of a rumour that the Royal Treasury is in something of a liquidity crisis.

**King**  Liquidity crisis? You talk in riddles, sir. What does that mean?

**Advisor**  The palace is up the creek?

**King**  I like this not. Send for the Royal Accountant.

**Advisor**  Very good, sire. (*calling out aloud*) The Royal Accountant.

**Lackey**  (*even more loudly*) Send for the Royal Accountant.

**King**  How goes my little chickadee?

**Advisor**  Princess Prudence?

**King**  No other.

**Advisor**  Milady is still ill of the strange mullet malady.

**King**  Are there no signs of improvement?

**Advisor**  I'm afraid not sire ... er ... (*musically*) the malady lingers on. (*Exits, stage right.*)

**King**  (*turning to the* **Wizard**) What do the heavens say, Wizard?

**Wizard**  Oh ... er ... um ... (*He takes out a telescope and looks up at the sky through it from the wrong end. The* **Royal Advisor** *helps him out by turning it the right way round. He then offers these rather unhelpful comments to the* **King**.) Er ... Venus is in transition.

**King**  Uh.

**Wizard**  And Mars is in conjunction with Jupiter.

**King**  Uh.

**Wizard**  But Mercury is in the ascendant.

**King**  Yes, but what does all this mean?

**Wizard** Either you are going to lose all of your hair or else you are going to be attacked by a dancing bear.

**King** What is your advice?

**Wizard** Do you know how to waltz?

**King** You imbecile. Is there nothing you can tell by looking at the skies?

**Wizard** (*looking up there again*) Hmmm . . . er . . . it's going to rain?

**King** What about my horoscope?

**Wizard** Just a minute. (*He takes a copy of a current magazine from his back pocket.*) Let me see. (*reading to himself*) Eleven best all-time knitting patterns, recipes for young mums on the move . . . er, you're a Pisces aren't you?

**King** Yes.

**Wizard** Ah, here we are.

**King** (*desperate*) What does it say?

**Wizard** It says, 'Don't listen to any superstitious advice'.

**King** That's the most sensible thing I've heard all year.

(***Lackey*** *sounds his trumpet to announce the arrival of the* ***Royal Accountant***.)

**Lackey** The Royal Accountant.

**Advisor** The Royal Accountant.

(***Accountant*** *clicks his heels to attract attention.*)

**King** Who are you?

**Accountant** Er . . . the Royal . . . er, Accountant, sire.

**King** Oh, you are are you? Well how do you account for the state of the royal finances? Or, failing that, as I'm sure you will, how do you account for the finances of the royal state?

**Accountant** (*trembling*) Er, I'm afraid we've reached a situation where our cash outflow has immensely exceeded our cash inflow, thus creating a huge deficit.

THE ROYAL ACCOUNTANT

**King** Come again?

**Accountant** We're spending too much money.

**King** Well, if that's all it is, it's easily fixed. Just ring up the Royal Mint and have them print up another batch ... er, ... of money, that is.

**Accountant** I'm afraid it's not that simple, sire.

**King** It's not? (**Accountant** *shakes his head*.) Well, there's only one thing for it, we have to cut down on expenses.

**Accountant** But we can't possibly trim the budget any more. Our war with Upper Slobovnia is costing us thousands every day.

**King** Tish, tosh. We all have to make some sacrifices. I myself will set the example by giving up spinach.

**Accountant** I'm afraid that won't be enough.

**King** Then we'll increase taxes.

**Accountant**  But sire, if we increase taxes any more the peasants will be paying more in tax than they earn in wages. Besides, we've already taxed everything we can think of: houses, land, horses, carts, horses and carts, walking, running, sitting, standing, living, dying. We have a travel tax, a poll tax, a departure tax and an arrival tax.

**King**  There must be something we can tax.

**Accountant**  But the peasants will hit the roof.

**King**  So what? We'll armour-plate the palace ceiling.

**Accountant**  No, I mean ...

**King**  (*interrupting*) How about a tax on tax?

**Accountant**  Ha, no peasant in his right mind would agree to that.

**King**  So, what's the problem? ... no peasant in his right mind would live in Lower Slobovnia.

**Accountant**  I cannot in all conscience agree to it.

**King**  Well, if you won't raise another tax for me you have only one last decision to make.

**Accountant**  Yes sire?

**King**  Would you prefer the gallows or the guillotine?

**Accountant**  But what good will come of my death?

**King**  We'll charge the peasants admission ... we'll make a fortune in hotdogs and flavoured milk. (*Rubs his hands in glee.*)

**Accountant**  Does this mean I'm fired?

**King**  If you want to take it that way.

(**Accountant** *exits, stage left.* **Royal Advisor** *enters, stage right.*)

**Advisor**  Your majesty, there are some peasants to see you.

**King**  We may make a double header of this yet.... What do they look like?

**Advisor**  Low foreheads, greasy hair, thick moustaches ...

**King**  They sound repulsive.

**Advisor**  The menfolk are even worse.... Their Spokesman demands an audience.

**King**  Why, what was he thinking of singing? ... Show the scoundrel in.

**Advisor**  (*calling in a loud voice*) The Spokesman of the Peasant Rebellion.

**Lackey**  The Spokesman of ...

**King**  You can skip that part.

**Peasant Spokesman**  (*forcing his way into the court*) We demand our rights.

**King**  Careful you saucy wretch, or the next rights you get may be your last.

**Peasant Spokesman**  (*suspiciously*) Are you the King?

**King**  No. (*Points to the **Lackey**.*) He's the King, I'm just keeping the throne warm for him. (***Spokesman** tries to interrupt.*) What did I do to deserve a subject like you? Take you hands out of your pocket ... and don't slouch. (***Spokesman** straightens up.*) Now, what is it that you want?

**Peasant Spokesman**  (*reading from a prepared speech*) We demand freedom of speech.

**King**  When was the last time I ever charged admission to one of my speeches?

**Peasant Spokesman**  We demand the right to bear arms.

**King**  Make a note, Lackey, to sell the peasants some singlets.

**Peasant Spokesman**  And we hereby give notice that we are beginning a hunger strike until the food shortage is brought to an end.

**King**  Hmmm, things have a way of working themselves out, don't they?

PEASANT SPOKESMAN

**Peasant Spokesman** *(continuing to read his petition)* And we the undersigned demand free public education for all peasants.

**King** What do you want to go to school for? ... Next thing you'll want to learn how to read and write.

**Peasant Spokesman** Here is the petition, signed by the peasants' collective of Lower Slobovnia. *(Hands the petition to the **King**.)*

**King** *(attempting to read the document)* But this handwriting is atrocious. I can't make out these signatures.

**Peasant Spokesman** I rest my case.

**King** Milton, throw this rogue in irons. And ring up the roundleaders of this rebellion ... er, you know what I mean.

**Advisor** Sire, if I might venture an opinion.

**King** What is it?

**Advisor** I do feel the peasants need something to occupy their minds.

**King** What about television?

**Advisor** It hasn't been invented yet.

**King** But what about my Life-Be-In-It activities? ... Dragon slaying, witch burning? All good clean fun.

**Advisor**   Yes, your grace, but it hasn't been a total success. Many of the peasants prefer giving themselves up to wine and women.

**King**   Revolting.

**Advisor**   Yes, that too.

(**Messenger** *hands note to* **Lackey**.)

**King**   Well, maybe the execution tomorrow will raise their spirits a little, eh?

**Lackey**   (*approaching the* **King**) Sire, I have been informed that this note has just arrived K.O.D. from Upper Slobovnia ... it arrived by carrier penguin.

**King**   K.O.D.?

**Lackey**   Kipper On Delivery.

**King**   Oh, I hope it's not another poison penguin letter.... Read it out.

**Lackey**   (*opening letter*) The writing's a bit blurred, sire. (*The paper is very soggy.*)

**King**   Try your best.

**Lackey**   Yes, sire. 'The King of Upper Slobovnia cordially offers the, er ... head ... er, ... hand of' ... it looks like 'Princess Slobov' ...

**Advisor**   Yes, that is the King's daughter.

**Lackey**   '... in marriage as a token of friendship, peace and mutual truffles between the two Slobovnias.'

**King**   Mutual truffles?

**Lackey**   (*rereading*) Er ... that must be 'mutual trust', the envelope must have leaked.

**King**   I wish someone would hurry up and invent the carrier pigeon.... So Walter wants peace at last. This is excellent, the old boy is loaded. We must dispatch a reply by penguin post immediately.

**Lackey**  I'm afraid we can't do that, sire.

**King**  Why not?

**Lackey**  Chef's speciality, penguin pie.

**King**  Er, go fetch Prince Egbert anyway. We've got to sell him on this Princess Slobov.

**Lackey**  Yes, your majesty.

(**Lackey** *exits, stage left.*)

**King**  We have to get in touch with Walter somehow. Wizard, can you suggest anything?

**Wizard**  Well, it just so happens I have been working on a device for making long-distance calls, but I haven't thought of a name for it yet.

**King**  Describe it.

**Wizard**  Well, the device brings voices from a long distance off much closer, rather like a telescope makes things look as if they are closer. And it translates sound waves into electrical currents, rather like a phonogram.

**King**  Well, isn't it obvious what you should call it? (**Wizard** *looks puzzled.*) Well, if it's half like a *tele*scope and half like a *phono*-gram ...

**Wizard**  Telescope ... and phonogram. Why, of course.

**King**  Yes?

**Wizard**  A scopogram.

**King**  (*looking disappointed*) Just bring it to me.

**Wizard**  (*quickly going off, stage right, to collect a telephone*) I haven't quite ironed out all the bugs yet either.

**King**  Never mind. (*He takes the telephone from the* **Wizard** *and begins dialling.*) Hello, King Walter ... (*Replaces the receiver in disgust.*) Wrong number.

**Wizard**  It's working perfectly. (*Exits, stage right.*)

**King** (*dialling again*) Hello, is that King Walter's residence? ... good.... Listen, I would have sent your penguin back, but unfortunately he died.... What of? ... er, malaria I think it was.... Listen, I got your note ... yeah, it was a little soggy. Yeah, we're definitely agreeable to it. Good ... then the marriage is definitely on. Send the little one down ... eight tonight. Great. Anyway, I've got to rush, bye now. (*Hangs up.*)

**Lackey** Prince Egbert, sire.

**Egbert** (*speaking with a pronounced lisp*) You withed to thee me, father?

**King** Yeth, ... er, I mean yes. Where have you been?

**Egbert** Down at the pond talking to the flowerth.

**King** What kind of a kook do I have for a son! You spent the whole day talking to a bunch of daisies?

**Egbert** Not jutht to the flowerth.

**King** Good.

**Egbert** I made friendth with a frog ath well.

**King** I should have guessed it.

**Egbert** Ath a matter of fact, I think I'm in love with her.

**King** In love with her? You are crazy.

**Egbert** Thee ith a printheth.

**King** I bet she says that to all the boys. You must have got this from your mother — no-one on my side of the family fell in love with any frogs.

**Egbert** Thee ith tho a printheth. Thee told me tho herthelf. All I have to do ith kith her and thee'll turn into one.

**King** Well, have you?

**Egbert** What kind of a boy do you think I am? We've only jutht met.

**King** Oh.

**Egbert** Bethideth, thee keepth thlipping out of my handth. I think I will athk her to marry me.

PRINCE EGBERT

**King**  Are you kidding? What kind of future could a frog have?

**Egbert**  You've obviouthly not heard of Kermit.

  (***Royal Advisor*** *exits, stage right.*)

**King**  But Princess Slobov of Upper Slobovnia wishes for your hand.

**Egbert**  (*looking at his hand*) Huh?

**King**  In marriage, dumb-dumb.

**Egbert**  Oh.... Well, that ith too bad. My hand and my heart belongth to Tricthie.

**King**  Oh, that's her name is it? Well, that's the craziest notion I've ever heard of, I absolutely forbid you to, er (*suddenly struck with an idea*) ... er.

**Egbert**  You were thaying, father?

**King** Yes, I ... er ... absolutely forbid you to keep her to yourself any longer. Why don't you ask her to come to the palace tonight ... about eight-fifteen, shall we say?

**Egbert** Ooooah, wonderful. I mutht thay, I didn't ecthpect you to approve.

**King** That's all right. Now run along and play with your train set.

(**Egbert** *exits, stage left.* **Advisor** *enters, stage right.*)

**Advisor** (*leading the* **Ringleader** *of the peasant rebellion in*) You asked for the ringleaders of the peasant rebellion, sire. Here is the principal leader.

**King** Very good, Milton. Read out the charges.

**Advisor** (*taking out a document*) Percival Blancmange-Pudding, you are hereby charged with High Treason, Low Treason and Middle Treason.

**King** In addition to sedition ...

**Advisor** Evasion of taxes, counterfeiting, forgery and operating a hotdog stand without a licence.

**King** Is there no end to your wickedness? How do you plead, knave?

**Ringleader** (*throwing himself before the* **King**) On my hands and knees?

**King** Have you no shame?

**Ringleader** Wait until you see me really grovel.

**King** Hold your tongue, dog.

**Ringleader** (*actually holding his own tongue*) Aaaaah eehhhha uuuuah aaay.

**King** What was that?

**Ringleader** (*releasing his tongue*) Whatever you say.

**King** Tell me, Milton, how does a man without talent, backbone or charm become a leader of men?

**Ringleader** You ought to know the answer to that one, King, baby ...

**King**  Why, you saucy rapscallion ... give me one reason why I shouldn't have your head.

**Ringleader**  Your crown wouldn't fit?

**King**  I ought to have you drawn and quartered.

**Ringleader**  That sounds painful.

**King**  It is.

**Ringleader**  Well, if it's all the same to you, I think I'll decline. I bruise very easily.

**King**  But I am a fair and a just man ... you will undergo trial by ordeal.

**Ringleader**  (*suspiciously*) What does that involve?

**King**  You will be bound in chains, taken to the banks of a fast-flowing river and tossed in. If you float, we will assume that the devil has intervened to save you and we will take you away to execute you; but if you drown, we will believe that you are perfectly innocent.

**Ringleader**  That sounds a trifle rigged ... is there another choice?

**King**  Only the coward's way.

**Ringleader**  That's more my style.

**King**  Lackey, the cards.

**Lackey**  Yes, sire. (*He takes out a pack of playing-cards.*)

**King**  There are fifty-two playing-cards here. Choose a king and you shall have a royal pardon. Choose any other and we execute you. (*Holds out the cards.*) Which do you choose?

**Ringleader**  That's easy ... I'll have the ... er ... king of spades.

(**Lackey** *takes out a rapier and presses it against the* **Ringleader***'s throat.*)

All right, already, just don't get pushy. (*He chooses a card. It is, of course, the wrong one.*)

PEASANT RINGLEADER

**King** (*seeing that it is the wrong card*) Good. Looks like we've got a double header tomorrow after all.... Boy, are we going to make a killing ... (**Ringleader** *looks glum.*) er ... sorry ... I meant on hotdogs.

**Ringleader** How about if I took back what I said about you? ... I'm too young to die.

**King** Too late.

**Ringleader** Come on, shake hands and make up ... I didn't mean all those nasty things I said about you ... promise, cross my heart and hope to die ... I mean ...

**King** Save your breath, you don't have much of it left.

**Ringleader** (*on his knees again*) Pretty please.

**King** With sugar on top?

**Ringleader**   And a cherry.

**King**   Sorry, I've already ordered the hotdogs.

**Ringleader**   Can't you even be bribed?

**King**   Did I say that?

**Ringleader**   How much?

**King**   Two hundred roubles.

**Ringleader**   That's outrageous . . . my uncle was ransomed for fifty.

**King**   The cost of living has gone up.

**Ringleader**   (*emptying his pockets to find some small change*) That's all I have.

**King**   Any last requests?

**Ringleader**   How about a South Pacific cruise?

**King**   Milton, escort this scum to the cells.

(**Royal Advisor** *drags out the struggling prisoner while he makes his final plea.*)

**Advisor**   Come on.

**Ringleader**   OK, a North Pacific cruise. I'm not fussy. A nice long trip down the Amazon, then.

**King**   Get out of here.

**Ringleader**   Come on. Let me go now and I'll forget all about it . . . I'm not one to hold a grudge.

(**Ringleader** *is taken off by the* **Royal Advisor**.)

**King**   Fetch the Wizard, will you, Lackey.

**Lackey**   Certainly, sire. (*Exits, stage left.*)

**Ringleader**   (*reappearing, stage right*) I'll never call you a nasty name again.

**King**   Be off with you.

(**Ringleader** *is collared by the* **Royal Advisor** *again.*)

**Ringleader**  Fishface!

(***Ringleader*** *is finally escorted right off the stage.*)

**King**  Oooh, that hurts.

**Lackey**  Sire, the Wizard says he'll be here in a flash.

**King**  Why can't he make a normal entry like everyone else? . . . Now to put my plan for Egbert into effect. Ah, my good Wiz.

**Wizard**  You summoned me, sire?

**King**  Ah, yes, indeed I did.

**Wizard**  What is it? The scopogram out of order?

**King**  No, no, nothing of the sort. I just want your help in a plan I have for getting my little Egbert to fall for Princess Slobov.

**Wizard**  Yes?

**King**  Well you see, I have told Egbert that he could invite his little frog girlfriend to the palace tonight at eight-fifteen.

**Wizard**  Yes?

**King**  But, though he doesn't know it, Princess Slobov will arrive at eight o'clock.

**Wizard**  Huh?

**King**  Now, all I want is for you to whip up a little love potion, so we can give it to Egbert when Princess Slobov arrives. When his beloved Trixie turns up, he'll have forgotten all about her.

**Wizard**  Yes, your lordship, that sounds like an excellent idea . . . except for one thing.

**King**  What's that?

**Wizard**  Love potions are not my line.

**King**  Not your line?

**Wizard**  No. I never was lucky in love, so to speak. Earthquakes, no trouble. Hurricanes, in a jiffy. Scopograms, . . . you name it. But love potions? . . . Not a sausage.

THE WIZARD

**King**   But what can I do? If I don't get my Egbert married off to Princess Slobov my kingdom is in ruin.

**Wizard**   So, who'll notice the difference?

**King**   (*menacingly*) And I'll have to axe some of my royal household.

**Wizard**   I see your point. (*Pauses to think for a moment.*) There was a witch I used to know, who went by the name of Lucrezia, who did specialize in love potions.

**King**   There was a witch you used to know? Who went by the name of Lucrezia? Who did specialize in love potions? Why didn't you say so?

**Wizard**   I thought I just did.

**King**   And how, might I ask, did you get to know this . . . er . . .

**Wizard**   Lucrezia Grimsky-Kharkov Wartchunkle was her name.

**King**   That's quite a mouthful.

**Wizard**  So were her love potions. We were in the same grade at Magic School. I usually topped the class in spells, but she always beat me in spelling.

**King**  She probably had plenty of practice on her surname. Where is she now?

**Wizard**  I heard she was thinking of setting up shop in the Enchanted Forest somewhere.

**King**  Well, don't shilly-shally. We need that potion. Get thee gone.

**Wizard**  (*bowing low*) Your wish is my command, sire. (*Exits, stage left. Lights fade.*)

## SCENE 2

*This scene is set in the dark interior of a forest. The lights are much lower. Lucrezia, bent over a cauldron, is stationed on the right-hand side of the stage, stirring the brew and reciting her spells with a very heavy Italian accent.*

**Lucrezia**  For a posh of bigga charm (*adding ingredients at random*)
Throwa inna halfa salaam.
Deada mousa and rotten fish
Makea up a lovely dish.
Garlic prawns and mouldy cheese,
Plentya pep to makea sneeze.
Uno momento not forget,
To adda in old spaghett.
Onea slicea used lasagna ... er ... lasagna ... lasagna ... (*searching for a word to rhyme with 'lasagna'*) campagna ... rhu-barbgna ... Hey Fishface. (*referring to the **Wizard**, who is standing by idly observing all this*) What rhymes for 'lasagna'?

**Wizard**  Er ... er ...

**Lucrezia**  Never minda, Fishface, I got it....
... And adda to a squashed banagna.

(*She adds the last ingredient to the broth.*)

LUCREZIA

**Wizard**  So what's cooking, Lucrezia?

**Lucrezia**  I makea uppa a big batcha love posh. (*pause*) How you knowa my name?

**Wizard**  I was in the same class as you at Magic School: Mrs Sycorax ... don't you remember me?

**Lucrezia**  Oh, yeah. I remember your fish, now.

**Wizard**  You mean you remember my face.

**Lucrezia**  I'm not so sure.... Well, it look like a fish.

**Wizard**  Well, weren't you voted Miss Rotund of the class of forty-four?

**Lucrezia**  Why you thinka I started up making the love posh?

**Wizard**  Didn't you leave school to start up your own fortune-telling business?

**Lucrezia**  That'sa right.

**Wizard**  What happened to that?

**Lucrezia**  I couldna see no future in it.

**Wizard**  What'd you do with your crystal ball?

**Lucrezia**  I painta she black and sella her for a bowling ball.

**Wizard**  You remember our class party that year?

**Lucrezia**  Yeah, you remember my pasta good?

**Wizard**  As if it were yesterday.

**Lucrezia**  No, nota my pasta ... my *pasta*.... Mamma mia, you makea me mad sometimes.... My pasta, I madea the macaroni.

**Wizard**  Oh, yes, I remember that. You always were a good cook, Lucrezia, I'll give you that.... How's the love potion coming along?

**Lucrezia**  (*stirring the base of the cauldron and scooping up some for the* **Wizard**) You wanta a taste?

**Wizard**  I'm not falling for that one.... What's the recipe for this?

**Lucrezia**  Oh, nothing spesh. I just throw up anything.

**Wizard**  You mean throw *in* anything.

**Lucrezia**  That's what I said, Fishface. But mainly just pizza.

**Wizard**  Pizza?

**Lucrezia**  Yeah. Pizza this, pizza that. Who cares? ... What for you want the posh anyway?

**Wizard**  Well, you see, the King wants his son, Prince Egbert, to marry Princess Slobov of Upper Slobovnia, but he's not interested. He's dating some floozy frog from down at the pond. So he wants a potion to make sure that when Egbert sets eyes on the Princess it'll be love at first sight.

**Lucrezia**  When doesa your King wanta thisa posh by?

**Wizard**  Well, Princess Slobov is due to arrive at the palace at eight o'clock tonight. . . .

**Lucrezia**  Ah, bellissima, I likea the love story. I give you some of thisa batch. It'sa finished the curdling, I mean the cooking, by now. (*Takes a vial and fills it up.*) Takea she free ofa the charges.

**Wizard**  Thanks Lucy, toodle loo.

**Lucrezia**  Arrivederci, Fishface. (*stirring the pot*)
Boila uppa a bigga lot
Posha in the bigga pot.

(*Lights come slowly up, stage left, where* **Egbert** *and* **Trixie** *are wandering through the Enchanted Forest.* **Trixie**'s *complexion is entirely green.*)

**Trixie**  (*in a teenage American accent*) Oh gee golly gosh, I knew we should have taken that last turn to the left. Now we're well and truly lost. Boo hoo. How are we ever going to find Lucrezia now? Boo hoo.

**Egbert**  Oh Tricthie, don't cry. You know how that tugth at my heart thtringth. (*He looks around the Forest.*) Letth athk that witch over there. (*They both look at* **Lucrezia**, *then suddenly give each other startled glances.*)

**Trixie**  Which?

**Egbert**  (*placing a finger on her lips to silence her*) Don't thay it. (*He walks over to* **Lucrezia**.) Ecthcuthe me, thir/madam, but you wouldn't by chanth happen to be Lucrethia?

**Lucrezia**  Who she is?

**Trixie**  (*walking over to join them*) He means Lucrezia, don't you honeybunch?

**Egbert**  Yeth, glamourputh.

**Lucrezia**  You gotta something bad wronga with your mouth, kiddo. Yeah, Lucrezia atsa me all right. Lucrezia Grimsky-Kharkov Wartchunkle. Atsa some name, huh? And who are you?

**Egbert**  I am Printhe Egbert, and thith ith my beloved, Tricthie.

**Lucrezia**  You pretty bigga for a frog, baby.

**Egbert**  But how did you know thee wath a frog?

**Lucrezia**  A lucky guess.

**Ebgert**  I don't believe you.

**Lucrezia**  Listen Eggplant, I don't have to tell you.... But since you ask anyway, I hearda it on the rumour.

**Egbert**  Well it doethn't matter anyway, becauth I kithed her and turned her into a Printheth.

**Trixie**  (*chewing a wad of gum*) But there were complications.

**Egbert**  Yeth, ath you can thee, thee thtill hath a green complecthion. And I'm afraid my father would never conthent to allow a blueblood to marry a greenthkin. The very idea would be prepothtereth.

**Trixie**  What Eggie-Weggie is trying to say is, have you got anything to cure green skin?

**Lucrezia**  (*fetching up a canister from behind the cauldron*) Thisa is all I got.

**Trixie**  (*rubbing a little between her thumb and forefinger*) What do you do with it?

**Lucrezia**  Rubba it in the face ... with steela woola.

**Trixie**  OK.

**Lucrezia**  (*handing over the canister*) One rouble.

**Egbert**  (*finding the money in his money-pouch*) What egthactly ith thith?

**Lucrezia**  Oh, she is old Gypsy recipe.

**Egbert**  What do you call it?

**Lucrezia**  Ajax.

**Trixie**  Yeah, but how can I be sure it'll work?

**Lucrezia**  I tella you whatta. If it doena work you give me all of it you gotta left back and I give you alla your money I got left back.

**Trixie**  Gee, that sounds swell. How can you afford to run a business like that, though?

**Lucrezia**  Ah, I was younga and greena myself once.

**Egbert**  You're really a good witch, Lucrethia.

**Lucrezia**  Don't let it get around, Eggflip. You'lla ruin my image.

**Trixie**  Anyway, we've got to run. We'll catch you later Lucy, so long.

**Egbert**  Yeth, cheerio. (*Trixie and Egbert exit, stage left. They don't go all the way offstage, though, but come to a point downstage left, approximately opposite that of* **Lucrezia**.)

**Lucrezia**  Arrivederci, I hopa you getta your mouth fixed upa soon. (*Continues stirring the pot, occasionally sampling some of the potion.*) Not bad kidsa. (*Samples some of the broth.*) Needsa more garlic ... (*Samples some more broth.*) Lika my Aunt Esmerelda saida to mea when I was a little bambina. You cannot do tooa many good deeds, just likea you cannot havea too mucha garlic ina the cookpot. (*pause*) Maybe ... no, I not interfere ... well, not verrar mucha anyway.... Maybe, I can dress up as Princess Slobov. (*Lights go up on* **Egbert** *and* **Trixie**.)

**Egbert**  (*pointing to* **Trixie**, *who has evidently come up with the same idea as* **Lucrezia**) You dreth up ath Printheth Thlobov?

**Trixie**  Sure, and why not? I am a real princess anyway.

**Lucrezia**  (*to herself*) And noa-one around here really knows what she looksa like.

**Trixie**  (*to Egbert*) No-one around here knows what she really looks like. (**Lucrezia** *and* **Trixie** *now speak simultaneously.*)

**Lucrezia and Trixie**  (*in their respective accents*) I'll go to the palace tonight dressed in my best clothes. No-one will be able to say that I'm not the Princess ... they'll have to believe me.

**Egbert**  And then when I drink the love pothion, I'll fall in love with you alone and there'll be nothing they can do about it.

**Lucrezia**  (*suddenly notices a flaw in her plan*) But whena Eggnoodle drinka the posha, he willa fall in lovea with me.... No, that'sa not right. (*pause*) I know, I swappa the posha and pretend to drinka it myself.... Then I takea them both back here so he can marra the frog just likea in the faira tale. (*Samples the broth.*) Needsa more garlic.


## SCENE 3

*The Palace. The **King** is pacing up and down delivering a speech while the **Royal Advisor** stands to one side of the throne with a glazed expression on his face.)*

**King**  I am at my wits' end. The war with Upper Slobovnia goes not well. They treat my threats with disdain, my demands with contempt, my warnings with laughter and my penguins with tomato sauce. Why, just the other day they brazenly invaded the flagship of the Royal Slobovnian Navy and stole both the paddles. And then, to add insult to injury, they went and kicked down a neat sand-castle we were building. I ought to have them drawn and quartered. I ought to have them guillotined. I ought to have them keelhauled. I ought ... to have ... some food! (*Returns to the throne a little subdued.*) What's on the dinner menu, Milton?

**Advisor**  (*taking out his dinner menu and reading*) Hotdogs.

**King**  But I don't feel like any more hotdogs.

**Advisor**  Sorry sire, they were left over from yesterday's execution.

**King**  What flavours have you got?

**Advisor**  (*reading the menu*) Thirty-four taste sensations. Boysenberry, pistachio, jaffa, lime, rockmelon, choc chip, butterscotch, Jamaican rum ...

**King**  OK, get me a lime hotdog ... er ... with peanut-butter, gherkins and onion.

**Advisor**  (*writing the order down*) Will that be all, sire?

**King**   Oh, get me a strawberry and sardine milkshake to go with the meal. (*Advisor snaps his fingers and the* **Lackey** *comes onstage to accept the order.*) I want something to settle my stomach. My tummy gets very upset in this job sometimes, I know I should never have taken it on in the first place. I wanted to be a peasant as a lad — nothing to worry about but starvation, famine and the occasional plague. But no, my mother wouldn't hear of it. 'Be a King,' she said, 'that's where all the money is.' And the careers advisor backed her up. They didn't tell me about the ulcers, the long hours and the hands callused from counting money all day long. (*The* **Advisor**, *bored by this long-winded speech, is starting to drop off to sleep.*) But you know the worst part of this job? No-one ever listens to me, that's the worst part. It's bad enough that my enemies pay no attention to my demands, but must my friends ignore me as well?

**Advisor**   (*suddenly waking up*) Huh?

**King**   It must be nearly time for my weekly speech.

**Advisor**   I thought that was it, sire.

**King**   Is all in readiness?

**Advisor**   (*taking some cottonwool out and stuffing it in his ears*) Just a moment, sire.

**King**   (*taking the cottonwool away from the* **Advisor**) I mean are the peasant multitudes ready?

**Advisor**   (*under his breath*) I doubt it.

**King**   Then show them in.

**Advisor**   Very well, your majesty. (*Claps his hands twice and the* **Lackey** *brings in two* **Peasants**.)

**King**   This is a peasant multitude?

**Advisor**   Cost-cutting measure by the Royal Accountant. These two men are condemned to life imprisonment for jaywalking.

**King**   Life, for jaywalking? That seems a little tough.

**Advisor**   They'd just snatched the entire take of the Royal Hotdog Stand at the time.

ROYAL ADVISOR

**King**    Oh, I see. Well, I'll give them a speech on how to mend their evil ways, and if they listen closely I'll reverse their sentence.

**Peasant 1**    All we have to do is listen to your speech? (***King*** *nods his head*.)

**Peasant 2**    Do we get a choice?

**Peasant 1**    Don't listen to Zeke, he's only kidding.

**King**    (*standing on a crate placed there by the* ***Royal Advisor***) Mend your evil ways, brethren, before it is too late. For too often, too late do we weigh up the consequences of our evil ... er ... ways. And evil sticks in the craw of even the mightiest throat. And gather ye neither sticks nor stones. For a rolling stone gathers no moss. And neither should we cast stones upon the outcast and the fallen ... er ... when they have been cast out or fallen down. For we ourselves, brothers, have fallen upon hard times. But let us remember that time waits for no man. And no man is an island unto himself. Thank you for your attention.

TWO PEASANTS

**Peasant 1**  What was that about?

**Peasant 2**  About five sentences too long ... something about no stone being an island.

**King**  I hope you have profited by this sermon.

**Peasant 2**  Wait, there might be something in this yet.

**King**  And may the Lord have mercy on your souls.... Take these peasants to the block.

**Peasant 1**  Hey, wait a minute. I thought you said you'd reverse our sentence.

**King**  And what was your sentence?

**Peasant 1**  Life.

**King**  Good, now you've got death. Are the hotdogs in readiness, Milton?

**Advisor**  Indeed they are, sire. (*Claps his hands and the* **Lackey** *comes to remove them.*)

**King**  Now, where is my wizard?

**Advisor**  He awaits your pleasure even now, sire.

**King**  Well, there's precious little of that.... Send him in.

**Advisor**  Yes, sire. (*Clicks his fingers and the **Wizard** enters, stage left.*)

**King**  And where's my dinner?

**Advisor**  I'll see what's holding it up, sire. (***Advisor** leaves, stage left.*)

**King**  Ah, my good Wizard. How did your quest go?

**Wizard**  Well sire, I did manage to find Lucrezia in the Enchanted Forest, and she gave me this vial of love potion (*holding up an empty perfume-bottle*) which I have taken the liberty of putting into this handy aerosol spraypak. (*Holds up the spray-can in his other hand.*)

**King**  Good work.

**Wizard**  The merest sniff and Egbert will fall madly in love with Princess Slobov.

**King**  And the Kingdoms of Upper and Lower Slobovnia will at last be united in matrimony.

**Advisor**  (*entering, stage left*) Your milkshake, sire. I'm afraid the royal cook burnt your hotdog.

**King**  It's a wonder he didn't burn the milkshake as well. Tell him to report to the Royal Stake in the morning. We'll give him a taste of his own medicine.

**Advisor**  Yes, sire.

**King**  Oh, and ask him whether he likes his stakes rare, medium or well done.

**Advisor**  Yes, sire.

**King**  Oh, and send for Egbert. It will soon be upon the stroke of eight.

**Advisor**  Yes, sire.

**King**  Oh, and arrange for four goblets on a silver salver and a bottle of the Royal Plonk to be brought here with all speed.

LACKEY

**Advisor**   (*finally getting a chance to leave*) Yes, sire.

**King**   (*to the* **Wizard**) Are you sure this spray will be effective?

**Wizard**   I've never known one of Lucrezia's to be defective.

**King**   It needs but one whiff?

**Wizard**   But the merest sniff.

**King**   To set the heart aching?

**Wizard**   Not to mention breaking.

**King**   For on whomever one gazes?

**Wizard**   For whomever's face one fazes.

**King**   Enough of this childish prattle. (*The* **Lackey** *has arrived with the goblets and plonk.*) Yes, Lackey, just leave them there.

**Lackey**  Yes, sire. (*Departs, stage left.*)

**King**  Young Egbert has but this plonk to taste, (*spraying the love potion into one of the goblets*) gaze on Slobov, then marry her in haste. (*The* **Royal Advisor** *arrives, accompanying* **Prince Egbert.**)

**Egbert**  Father, you thummoned me?

**King**  Yes, my royal eggling, there is someone I would like you to meet.

**Egbert**  Who ith it?

**King**  Someone very special.

**Egbert**  Yeth?

**King**  Thee will be — I mean, she will be here at eight o'clock.

**Egbert**  Whoever could it be, father?
(*aside*) In ignoranth I'll feign to be,
When he revealth Tricthie to me.

**King**  Oh, just a girl.
(*aside*) Even if Slobov should prove a dog,
He'll still have to give up that frog.

**Egbert**  But you know that only one girl in the whole world interethtth me.

**King**  I won't have a son of mine running around with any old frog he's picked up at the local pond. It's downright unhealthy, apart from anything else. People are starting to talk. Think of the scandal. Think of the diseases!

**Lackey**  (*announcing*) Her Royal Highness of Upper Slobovnia, Princess Slobov.

**Advisor**  (*repeating the announcement*) Her Royal Highness of Upper Slobovnia, Princess Slobov.

**King**  But it's not yet eight o'clock. Oh well, never mind. (*Enter* **Lucrezia** *dressed as a princess.*)

**Egbert**  (*aside*) Oh no, Tricthie's planth have fallen amith,
I'd rather be beheaded than be wedded by thith.

**King**  Welcome to our humble court of Lower Slobovnia, your grace.
(*aside*) With legs like a jelly and arms like a sponge,
There's just desserts in calling her a human blancmange.

**Egbert**  May I be ecthcuthed, father?
(*aside*) Her form ith thertainly of ample proporthion:
To embrathe all of her would require thome contorthion.

**King**  No, you may not.
(*aside*) Such incredible bulk it would be hard to fill;
For her food alone I'd hate to foot the bill.

**Egbert**  I fcel I have a headache coming on, thir.
(*aside*) The real printheth early, my Tricthie late.
Thee thould have arrived by the thtroke of eight.

**King**  You would not think to offend our honoured guest, Egbert, I'm
sure. Have a little respect for Princess Slobov.

**Egbert**  I do have little rethpect for her.

**King**  I trust you had a pleasant journey, Princess Slobov.

**Lucrezia**  Thank ya plenty mucha. Boya I am plenty thirsty.

**King**  So you must be. Lackey, a drink for our guests.

**Lackey**  Yes, your majesty. (*The **Lackey** takes the tray around to the **King**
and the **Wizard**, who select their drinks; then to **Lucrezia**, who also
takes one. The last drink on the tray is **Egbert**'s.*)

**King**  Might I propose a toast, then ... (*raising his goblet*) An end to
the warfare between our two nations. (*They all raise their goblets.*)

**Lucrezia**  Hold it, everaone. Upper Slobovnian custom. We musta
eacha swappa the glassa.

**King**  (*aside*) Who drinks the potion, princess or prince,
Matters little if they end up kins.
Yes, very well then. Why don't you swap with Egbert, and I'll
swap with the Wizard.

**Lucrezia**  Atsa exactly what I gonna say. (*They swap goblets.*) Phew!
(*muttering under her breath*) Too mucha garlic.

**King**  Princess Slobov?

**Lucrezia** Oh, I say, nice wine. You musta give me the recip sometime.

**King** It's pretty simple. Just grapes and dirty feet.

**Lucrezia** (*aside*) I musta holda this to my lip,
But noa wine musta I sip.

(*The* **King** *pushes* **Egbert** *forward a little.*)

**King** And so, Princess, what think you of our noble son Egbert?

**Lucrezia** A bit on the skinny sida, isn't he?

**King** (*to the* **Wizard**) It's a bit slow in working, isn't it?

**Wizard** (*to the* **King**) But Lucrezia assured me it was her finest batch.

**King** And what do you think, Egbert, of Princess Slobov?

**Egbert** Thomewhat rotund thire, think you not?

**King** Think of the advantages: warmth in winter, shade in summer.

**Wizard** I'm afraid it looks quite hopeless, sire. Egbert stands amazed, but not enraptured. And the Princess herself looks most displeased.

**Lackey** (*announcing*) Her Royal Highness, Princess Slobov of Upper Slobovnia?

**Advisor** (*repeating the announcement*) Her Royal Highness, Princess Slobov of Upper Slobovnia? (*Enter, stage left,* **Trixie** *in a princess costume.*)

**King** What means this strange occurrence?

**Trixie** I am Princess Slobov.

**King** No thanks, we already have one of them. Couldn't you be someone else?

**Egbert** (*aside*) Too late doth my Tricthie appear.

**Lucrezia** (*aside*) Mamma mia, the froga is here.

**King** Methinks there's something rotten in the state of Upper Slobovnia.

TRIXIE

**Lucrezia**  Upper Upper Slobovnia or Lower Upper Slobovnia?

**King**  I didn't know there was a difference.

**Lucrezia**  Oh sure, there'sa bigga difference. Thatsa where your problem is. I am Princess Slobov from Upper Upper Slobovnia, and *she* is Princess Slobov from Lower Upper Slobovnia. Then again, I coulda come from the upper part of Upper Upper Slobovnia and she coulda come from the lower part of Lower Upper Slobovnia, or vicea versa. But I haven't got the breath to explaina the wholla thing to you.

**King**  Oh. (*pause*) But who is it, you or she, who wishes to marry Egbert?

**Lucrezia**  That skinny runt? You musta kid me. It musta be thisa other chick. (*Points to* **Trixie**.)

**Trixie**  (*not completely understanding what has gone on*) Yes, it is I. But only if Prince Egbert is a willing party to the arrangement.

**Egbert**  (*swooning*) Oh yeth. Goodie gumdropth.

**King**  He does not seem too displeased. Well, now at last we're all agreed. Let's solemnize our vows with speed. (*Trixie* and *Egbert extend their hands towards the* **King**, *who places them in his own clasp.*)

**Lackey**  My Lord, the state coach of Upper Slobovnia approaches.

**King**  Your eyes must deceive you, Lackey, for both princesses are already here.

**Lackey**  No, I assure you, 'tis true.

**King**  A veritable plethora of princesses, I see. Milton, see what's up. (***Advisor** leaves.*)

**Trixie**  (*aside*) Alas, I fear I am undone.

**Egbert**  (*aside*) The real Printheth Thlobov yet doth come,
If thee be half the firtht, then I am done.

**Advisor**  (*announcing*) Prince— (*He is cut off by the* **King**.)

**King**  I know, another Princess Slobov of Upper Slobovnia. (***Prince Slobov** strides into the room.*)

**Advisor**  No, *Prince* Slobov of Upper Slobovnia.

**King**  Oh, Prince Slobov ... er ... we thought you were your sister ... er ... that is to say, we thought you were a princess. (***Prince Slobov** isn't very impressed by this statement.*) Er ... but of course, your sister is standing over there. (*The* **King** *points to* **Trixie**, *who shrinks away nervously.*)

**Prince Slobov**  But that is not my sister — though I wish I had a sister as pretty as she. My sister is fat and ugly.

**King**  Oh, you're from Upper Upper Slobovnia, then? ... There is your sister over there. (*Points to* **Lucrezia**.)

**Prince Slobov**  But that is not my sister either.

**King**  (*exasperated*) Oh, come now. One of these two must be your sister. Make up your mind which one.

**Prince Slobov**  Neither. I left my sister in Upper Slobovnia after receiving your letter by carrier penguin. I came here in expectation of marrying *your* princess.

**King**  *Our* princess?

**Prince Slobov**  (*with a heroic rippling of the chin-muscles*) Yes.

**King**  Princess Prudence?

**Prince Slobov**  I know of no other.

**King**  I *hope* there's no other.... How is the good princess today, Milton?

**Advisor**  Feeling much better, sire.

**King**  Good, then fetch her hither.

**Advisor**  (*not understanding*) Her hither, sire?

**King**  Bring her here!

**Advisor**  Oh. (*The **Advisor** dispatches the **Lackey** to get **Prudence**.*)

**King**  (*to **Prince Slobov***) But did not your father's message say that he offered the hand of Princess Slobov in marriage?

**Prince Slobov**  No.

**King**  Curious.

**Wizard**  Sire, if I might venture an opinion.

**King**  Yes?

**Wizard**  Perhaps the two esses at the end of 'Princess' washed away when the envelope leaked.

**King**  Yes, that is a possibility.... But what of these two extra princesses here now? How do we explain them?

**Lucrezia**  Oh yeah, I been meaning to talka to you abouta thisa.

**King**  You are an impostor?

**Lucrezia**  No, I'ma Lucrezia. You gottat no righta calla me a liar just because I not tella the truth.

PRINCESS PRUDENCE

**King**  Why not?

**Lucrezia**  Because I did it for my friends here, Eggplant and the frog.

**King**  Frog?

**Trixie**  I'm not really a frog, sire.

**Lucrezia**  You oughta see her catcha the mosquitoes.

**Lackey**  (*interrupting their conversation*) Her Royal Grace, Princess Prudence.

**King**  (*to **Trixie***) I'll get back to you later. Frog indeed!

**Princess Prudence**  (*in dressing-gown*) Father? You called for me?

**King**  Yes, my dear. How are you feeling?

**Princess Prudence**  Much better, thank you.

**King**  Oh, Prudence, I would like you to meet a visitor from Upper Slobovnia. Prince . . . (***Prince Slobov*** *executes a low bow and kisses her hand.*)

PRINCE SLOBOV

**Princess Prudence**  Charming.

**King**  No, Slobov. Prince Slobov seeks your hand in marriage.

**Princess Prudence**  Doesn't he want the rest of me too?

**Prince Slobov**  Indeed.

**King**  Good, that's settled at last. Our two kingdoms will be united in the holy bond of matrimony.... Now, about this frog of yours, Egbert.

**Egbert**  Thee ithn't really a frog, daddy.

**Trixie**  Let me handle this, Eggflip. No, indeed not, sir. For I am truly the daughter of the King of Fairyland, and therefore a real princess.

**King**  I'll go along with it so far.

**Trixie**  Anyway, I was changed into a frog by the evil witch of the north wood. I am sure my own father will amply reward Egbert when he learns that it was he who bestowed the kiss which transformed me from a frog into the beautiful, noble, gracious, sweet, kind, lovable, gentle, even-tempered, thrifty — er, did I mention beautiful? . . .

**King**  I think it was in there somewhere.

**Trixie**  . . . beautiful and modest girl you see before you now.

**King**  At this stage I'll buy anything. Well, I can't think of any objection off hand to having an amphibian in the family. But as for you, Lucrezia . . .

**Lucrezia**  You talka to me?

**King**  Yes. As for you, I can see that you were interested more in protecting your friends than yourself. For that you deserve our reward, not our anger. Name one thing you desire and it shall be yours.

**Lucrezia**  Justa likea thatta?

**King**  Just like that. (**Lucrezia** *fixes a long, lustful gaze on the* **Wizard**.)

**Lucrezia**  I musta say I would likea someonea to calla my owna. . . . (*shyly*) Someone to sharea my spaghetti bolognese witha me.

**King**  Wizard?

**Wizard**  (*taking out his can of aerosol love potion*) She is a good cook, sire. (*He sprays the can in the air and they kiss under the cloud of vapour.*)

**Lucrezia**  Much too mucha garlic.

*CURTAIN*

KING JEROME

## Questions

1 In what way does the title, *A Star Is Spawn,* suggest that the play is likely to be a humorous one?

2 What important task does the Narrator perform for the reader as the play opens?

3 How does the King react to the news that his kingdom is tottering on the brink of collapse?

4 What advice is offered by the Wizard to the King?

5 The King receives a letter from Upper Slobovnia. How is it delivered? What does it offer?

6 What is a 'scopogram' and how did it get its name?

7 What unusual habits does the young Prince Egbert display?

**8** Why does the wizard go to the Enchanted Forest?

**9** What is unusual (and funny) about the spell Lucrezia chants as she stirs her cauldron?

**10** Explain the humour in the following exchange:
*Wizard:* Didn't you leave school to start up your own fortune-telling business?
*Lucrezia:* That'sa right.
*Wizard:* What happened to that?
*Lucrezia:* I couldna see no future in it.

**11** What happened when the Prince kissed the frog he was in love with?

**12** What was the complication?

**13** What comment do you have to make about the King's taste in hotdogs and milkshakes?

**14** How do the two peasants who have been given life imprisonment for jaywalking react to the King's speech on how to mend their evil ways?

**15** Why is Egbert going to be given a sniff of the love potion?

**16** Explain how the marriages of the following people are finally sorted out: Prince Egbert, Prince Slobov, Trixie, Princess Prudence.

# THE CANTERVILLE GHOST

## Tom Hayllar

(Adapted from the story by Oscar Wilde)

---

### Cast

**Narrator**
**Lord Canterville,** *the aristocratic owner of Canterville Castle.*
**Mr Hiram B. Otis,** *the American millionaire who buys Canterville Castle.*
**Mrs Otis,** *his wife.*
**Washington,** *their eldest son.*
**Virginia,** *their daughter.*
**Stars**
**Stripes** } *their terrible twin sons — noted for their practical joking.*
**Mrs Umney,** *the housekeeper of Canterville Castle.*
**Sir Simon de Canterville,** *the frightful ghost of Canterville Castle since 1584.*
**Spirit**
**Headless Skeleton** } *Sir Simon's dreadful assistants.*

*SCENE 1  Lord Canterville's London office.*

**Narrator**  When Hiram B. Otis, who is a real live millionaire from the good old U.S. of A., decided to buy the magnificent but gloomy Canterville Castle, everyone told him he was doing a very foolish thing. Why? Well, there was no doubt at all that the place was haunted. Even Lord Canterville, the owner, told him that. . . .

**Lord Canterville**  We have not lived in Canterville Castle since my grand-aunt, the Duchess of Bolton, was frightened into a fit from which she never fully recovered, by two skeleton hands placed on her shoulders as she was dressing for dinner.

**Mr Otis**  Pure hallucination!

**Lord Canterville**  The ghost has been seen by several living members of my family, and also by the rector of the parish.

**Mr Otis**  They were probably all drunk at the time.

**Lord Canterville**  Lady Canterville, who drinks only tea, has heard mysterious noises coming from the corridors and the library of the castle.

**Mr Otis**  Rats!

**Lord Canterville**  I fear . . .

**Mr Otis**  (*impatiently*) We Americans come from a modern country. If your ghost turns up in my castle I'll trap him and cage him and give him his own sideshow at a circus.

**Mrs Otis**  That's the spirit, Hiram!

**Lord Canterville**  But the ghost *does* exist. This has been well known for three centuries, since 1584 in fact, and it always appears just before the death of a member of our family.

**Mr Otis**  Well, for that matter, so does the family doctor.

**Mrs Otis**  Ghosts do *not* exist.

**Lord Canterville**  When the ghost does appear, just remember I warned you.

**Mr Otis**  That's settled then. We'll move in tomorrow. There's my wife, whom you've met. Then there's my eldest son Washington, and my daughter Virginia —

**Washington and Virginia**  Hi, Lord.

**Lord Canterville**  Er, hi.

**Mr Otis**  And last but not least, meet my terrible twins. This one's called Stars and this one's called Stripes. Say howdy to the lord, boys.

**Stars**  Aw, shucks!

**Stripes**  Aw, phooey!

**Lord Canterville**  Howdy — I mean, how do you do. (*turning to Mr Otis*) Why are they called Stars and Stripes?

**Mr Otis**  Well, when I get through swishing them and belting them for their practical joking, they see stars and they look like stripes.

**Lord Canterville**  I can't wait for them to meet the horrible apparition that we call the Canterville Ghost.

SCENE 2  *Canterville Castle — the library.*

**Narrator**  The Otis family drive to Canterville Castle. At first it is sunny, but as they approach the castle the sky becomes overcast and gloomy, a great stillness falls upon the countryside, and a flock of black birds passes silently over their heads. As they reach the castle, rain begins to fall.

**Mr Otis**  Well, at least there's somebody out on the steps to welcome us.

**Narrator**  Standing on the steps is an old woman dressed in black. It is Mrs Umney, the housekeeper.

**Mrs Umney**  (*in a solemn voice*) I bid you welcome to Canterville Castle. Tea is served in the library. Please follow me. (*They enter the library.*) Milk and sugar?

**Mrs Otis** (*interrupting, pointing to the fireplace*) Good heavens, what's that terrible red stain near the fireplace? Something has been spilt there.

**Mrs Umney** Yes, ma'am, blood has been spilt on that spot.

**Virginia** (*horrified*) How awful!

**Mrs Otis** Well, I don't like the look of bloodstains in any room. It must be removed at once.

**Mrs Umney** You don't understand. It is the blood of Lady Eleanore de Canterville, who was murdered on that very spot by her own husband, Sir Simon de Canterville, in 1575. Sir Simon remained for nine years, then disappeared suddenly under very mysterious circumstances. His body has never been discovered but his guilty spirit still haunts the castle. The bloodstain has been much admired by tourists and others, and cannot be removed.

**Washington** That's all rubbish! Pinkerton's Champion Stain Remover and Paragon Detergent will clean it up in no time.

(**Washington** *rushes out and returns with a bottle. He falls on his hands and knees and scours the floor.*)

There! I knew Pinkerton's would do the trick.

**Narrator**   Just as the stain is removed there is a peal of thunder, and a terrible flash of lightning illuminates the sombre room.

**Mr Otis**   (*calmly*) What an annoying climate this country has.

**Mrs Umney**   (*trembling*) It's not only the stain, sir. I've seen things with my own eyes that would make anyone's hair stand on end. Many a night I've not closed my eyes in sleep for the awful things that are done here.

**Mrs Otis**   (*anxiously*) You won't leave us, will you Mrs Umney?

**Mrs Umney**   I wish I could stay, ma'am, but there *is* the ghost, and my wages ...

**Mrs Otis**   I'll double them.

**Mrs Umney**   (*brightening*) Why thank you, ma'am.

**Mr Otis**   Now, I think we should all get a good night's rest. (*They all go out and to bed.*)


SCENE 3   *The library; the bedrooms.*

**Narrator**   Several evenings have passed without any sign of the ghost. Now, just before going to bed, the Otis family is once more gathered in the library. Washington is staring at the stain near the fireplace and scratching his head.

**Washington**   Well, so far the ghost hasn't shown himself, but that wretched stain keeps on coming back every time I clean it off. I've tried using everything on it, so it can't be the fault of the Paragon Detergent or Pinkerton's Champion Stain Remover.

And do you know, it's been a different colour every morning — first a dull red, then a rich purple, and this morning it was a bright green. It can't be anything else. It must be the ghost.

**Mr Otis**  I hate to admit it but you're probably right. I locked the library myself with a key. Who else but a ghost could get in?

**Mrs Otis**  Time for bed again. Let's all go upstairs and get a good night's rest.

**Narrator**  The family retires at eleven o'clock, and by half-past all the lights are out.... Some time later, Mr Otis in his room and the twins in theirs are awakened by a curious noise in the corridor.

**Mr Otis**  What was that? (*He sits up in bed. In the other room the twins wake.*)

**Stars**  Heck. Something just woke me up.

**Stripes**  Me too. Sounds like the clank of metal.

**Stars**  And it's coming closer.

**Stripes**  Let's look.

**Mr Otis**  I'm going to see what all that noise is. (*He picks up a little bottle.*) I'll just take this with me.

**Narrator**  Mr Otis and the twins open their doors and look out into the corridor. In the moonlight they see a terrible old man. His eyes are as red as burning coals. Long grey hair falls over his shoulders in matted coils. His ancient garments are soiled and ragged. From his wrists and ankles hang heavy manacles and rusty chains. The end of one of the chains is held by a pale spirit with purple eye-sockets, while the end of another chain is twisted in the bony fingers of a headless skeleton. These two figures are obviously assistants to the terrible ghost of Sir Simon de Canterville.

**Mr Otis**  (*addressing the ghost*) My dear sir, I really must insist that you — or one of your assistants — oil your chains and get rid of that frightful clanking noise they make when you drag them along. To help you out, I'll give you this small bottle (*showing the bottle*) of Rising Sun Lubricator. It should give complete satisfaction — but if it doesn't there's a money-back guarantee. I'll leave it here by these candles, and if you need any more I'll be happy to supply you. (**Mr Otis** *goes back into his bedroom.*)

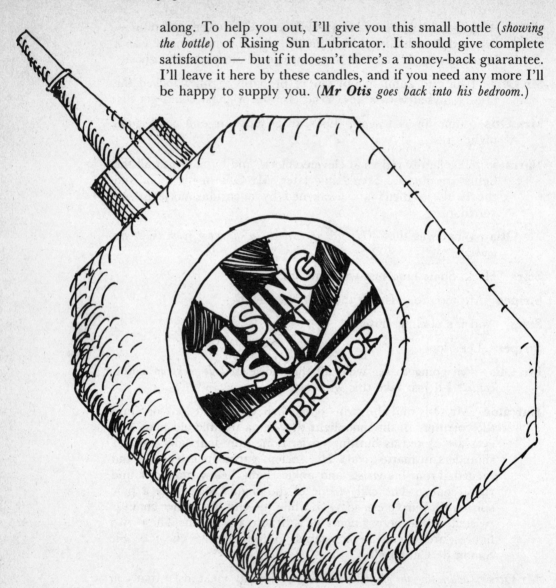

**Narrator**   For a moment the ghost stands still, the spirit opens and closes its mouth silently and the skeleton scratches its ribs. Then Sir Simon grabs the bottle and smashes it on the floor.

Next he and his assistants storm down the corridor uttering hollow groans and giving out flashes of ghastly green light. However, as they reach the twins' room, a nasty shock awaits them. . . .

**Stars**   Hey! It's a bunch of ugly ghosts!

**Stripes**   Let's hit them with the pillows! (*They hurl pillows at the ghosts.*)

**Narrator**   For Sir Simon and his assistants there is obviously no time to be lost. They vanish into the walls and the house becomes quiet.

*SCENE 4   A small secret chamber in the left wing of the castle.*

**Narrator**   Sir Simon and his assistants, in a gloomy mood, are leaning or sitting on moonbeams and talking about past triumphs.

**Sir Simon**   Never in my brilliant career of three hundred years have I been so grossly insulted. Those terrible twins — not like normal terrified children at all. And that bottle of . . . of lubricator!

**Spirit**   (*purple eyes rolling*) Think of all the people you've scared to death — or at least out of their wits. Remember how badly you frightened the Dowager Duchess when you cackled over her shoulder while she stood looking into her mirror?

**Headless Skeleton**   (*whose voice comes out from behind its breastbone*) You sent four housemaids into hysterics merely by grinning madly at them through the curtains of their bedroom windows.

**Sir Simon**   (*chuckling*) I'll never forget old Madame de Tremouillac. She woke up early one morning to see you, my dear Skeleton, seated in her armchair by the fire with your skull on your lap. She had to be confined to bed for six weeks with brain fever.

**Spirit**   (*purple eyes glowing with enthusiasm*) What a night it was when the butler shot himself in the pantry just because he saw my green fingers tapping at the window pane.

**Sir Simon**   And how about my appearances as 'Red Ruben' and as 'Gaunt Gideon, the Bloodsucker of Bexley Moor'? And how about the furore you caused one evening, my pale Spirit, simply by playing ninepins with Skeleton's bones out on the tennis-court?

**Narrator**   And after all this, a few wretched modern Americans have turned up and offered him Rising Sun Lubricator and thrown pillows at his head! It is unbearable. No ghosts in history have ever been treated like this . . . .

**Sir Simon**   I WANT REVENGE!


SCENE 5   *The bedrooms; the hall.*

**Narrator**   The second appearance of the ghost and his assistants takes place the very next night. Shortly after the Otis family have gone to bed, they are suddenly alarmed by a fearful CRASH in the hall . . . .

**Mr Otis**   What was that?

**Washington**   It came from downstairs. Let's go!

**Stars**   Bring your peashooter.

**Stripes**   I've got it — and the peas.

(*Meanwhile, downstairs in the hall* . . .)

**Sir Simon**   (*dazed*) What happened? Where am I?

**Spirit**   You were trying to get into your favourite suit of armour when it toppled over.

**Headless Skeleton**   Yes, and you bumped your head.

**Sir Simon**   (*groaning*) Help me over to a chair.

**Narrator**   Sir Simon is rubbing his bruised head when the Otis family burst into the hall.

**Mr Otis**   (*waving a revolver*) Hands up, all two and a half of you!

**Stars and Stripes**   (*peashooters to their mouths*) Ready, aim, FIRE!

**Sir Simon**   OUCH! OUCH! OUCH!

**Headless Skeleton** OOH — that went right through me!

**Spirit** OOF! I've been hit and my hand's turning green again!

**Narrator** But Sir Simon recovers swiftly and gives a wild shriek of rage, which turns into demoniac laughter....

**Sir Simon** EeeeeeeeeeEEEEECCCCHHHHHAAHAAHaahaahaha-HEEHEHeeheeheee!

**Narrator** This is Sir Simon's celebrated peal of demoniac laughter, which has never failed in three centuries. It is the very laugh which turned Lord Raker's wig grey in a single night. It once put two of Lady Canterville's French governesses in an asylum for life.

    Sir Simon is laughing as he mounts the stairs. Suddenly a door opens and Mrs Otis appears.

**Mrs Otis** EXCUSE ME! (**Sir Simon** *stops laughing. His mouth falls open.*) You are a sick man — er, ghost. That dreadful screaming suggests severe indigestion. I've brought you this bottle of Dr Dobell's Foaming Digestion Deterrent. I think you'll find it an excellent remedy. You might try giving some to *him*, too. (*She points to the* **Headless Skeleton**.)

FOAMING

DR. DOBELL'S
DIGESTION
DETERRENT

**Narrator**  The ghost glares at her in fury and at once prepares to turn himself into a huge black dog.

**Sir Simon**  (*furiously*) Here I come as the huge Black Dog!

**Spirit**  You're famous for it. Lord Canterville's uncle, the Honourable Thomas Horton, was terrified into permanent idiocy when you last made your appearance as the Black Dog.

**Narrator**  Sir Simon has got as far as turning black and hairy and falling on all fours when there is a sudden interruption. He looks up to see the Otis twins leaping towards him....

**Sir Simon**  Oh, no! What'll I do?

**Headless Skeleton**  Quick, the number-ten vanishing trick!

**Stars**  Grab him before he vanishes!

**Stripes**  I've got him! No! He's melting away — and becoming faintly phosphorescent!

**Sir Simon**  AAAAAAaaaaaahhhhhhuuuugggg!

**Narrator**  That was Sir Simon's deep and famous churchyard groan, which always accompanies the number-ten vanishing trick. The twins, however, are not impressed.

**Stars**  (*disgustedly*) The old coward has taken off.

**Stripes**  Yeah, and what a stupid sound he had to make as he was going.

SCENE 6  *Several nights later, in a small secret chamber in the*
*left wing of the castle.*

**Narrator**  Sir Simon and his assistants are in a happy mood. As they lean or sit on moonbeams, they make plans for the complete and final supernatural attack on the Otis family....

**Sir Simon**  (*singing*) Happy nights are here again.

**Headless Skeleton**  (*also singing*) The more we are together the happier we'll be.

**Spirit**  (*crooning*) Raindrops keep falling through my head.

**Sir Simon**  Tonight we strike! Tonight I will appear in my grisly guise of 'Jonas the Graveless'.

**Spirit**  (*enthusiastically*) Also known as 'The Corpse-Snatcher of Chertsey Barn'!

**Sir Simon**  Let me see ... the last time I gave such a horrible performance was in 1854. When old Lady Startup saw me creeping forward as Jonas that fatal New Year's Eve, she produced the most piercing of shrieks, which culminated in violent apoplexy and caused her to die in three days after disinheriting the Cantervilles and leaving all her money to charity.

**Headless Skeleton**  The weather is perfect for our venture. A storm is raging outside, the wind is howling and all the windows and doors are rattling.

**Sir Simon**  O bliss! O rapture! Tonight's the night. Now, here's the plan. (*The **Spirit** and the **Headless Skeleton** move close to **Sir Simon**.*) We will float noiselessly to the room of Washington Otis. Skeleton will wake him with the clutch of a bony hand and then the three of us will gibber at him from the foot of his bed. I will next stab myself three times in the throat ...

**Headless Skeleton**  (*eagerly*) While I provide slow music by tapping my skull gently against my spine.

**Sir Simon**  Well, he needs to be taught a lesson for continuously removing the famous Canterville bloodstain with Pinkerton's Paragon Detergent!

**Spirit**  That should reduce the reckless and foolhardy youth to a state of abject terror.

**Sir Simon**  Precisely. We will next proceed to the room occupied by Mr Otis and his wife. Once there, I will place a clammy hand on Mrs Otis's forehead, while ...

**Spirit**  I hiss into her trembling husband's ear the awful secrets of the grave.

**Sir Simon**  Who's next?

**Spirit** Young Miss Virginia.

**Sir Simon** Ah, yes. She has never insulted me in any way and she is pretty and gentle. A few hollow groans from the wardrobe, I think, will be more than sufficient for her. Or, if that fails to wake her, I may grabble at her sheets with palsy-twitching fingers. And now for the twins!

**Spirit and Headless Skeleton** Get the twins!

**Sir Simon** The first thing we'll do is sit on their chests so as to produce the stifling sensation of a nightmare. Then, as their beds are quite close together, I will stand between them in the form of a green, icy-cold corpse till they become paralysed with fear.

**Headless Skeleton** Meanwhile, I will crawl around the floor with white bleached bones in the character of 'The Suicide's Skeleton'.

**Spirit** And I will hover above their beds and, with rolling eyeballs, play the famous role of 'Martin the Maniac'.

**Narrator** At half-past ten they hear the family going to bed. For some time there are wild shrieks of laughter from the twins but, as midnight sounds, all is still and the three awful figures flit forth. On and on they glide while the rain and wind lash the castle. Every now and then Sir Simon mutters strange sixteenth-century curses and brandishes his rusty dagger in the air. . . .

**Spirit** Here is the passage that leads to the room of the luckless youth called Washington.

**Sir Simon** (*chuckling*) I can't wait to — OOOOOooooHHHHHaaaa-HHHHH!

**Narrator** Suddenly, with a piteous wail of terror, Sir Simon hides his blanched face in his long, bony hands. Right in front of him there stands a horrible spectre. Never having seen a ghost before, Sir Simon is naturally terribly frightened. . . .

**Sir Simon** (*trembling*) What — what do you want with me, O Spectre?

**Narrator**   The 'spectre' is really one twin seated on the other's shoulders. A sheet covers them both and a flashlight shining through two holes provides a nasty hypnotic glare.

**Spectre**   (*holding out a rolled sheet of paper*) Take this scroll. Read it and repent!

**Narrator**   Having pronounced these doom-filled words, the spectre backs through an open doorway and is gone forever.

**Headless Skeleton**   Phew — my bones are still rattling.

**Spirit**   What does the scroll say, Sir Simon?

**Sir Simon**   (*unrolling the paper*) It says: 'This scroll comes from ye olde Otis Ghoste, ye onlie true and originale spook. Beware of ye imitationes. All others are counterfeite.'

**Headless Skeleton**   That's spooky.

**Sir Simon**   No, No. It's worse than that!

**Narrator**   He suddenly realizes that he has been tricked — by the terrible Otis twins. He grinds his toothless gums together and, raising his withered hands high above his head, swears many horrible oaths.

**Spirit**   (*nervously looking around*) We must vanish . . .

**Headless Skeleton**   (*twitching*) In — in case the spectre should — should return.

**Narrator**   So the three of them vanish into the nearest wall and retire to restless sleep in comfortable lead coffins.

*SCENE 7   The lead coffins in the secret sleeping-chamber; the twins' bedroom.*

**Narrator**   It is the following day, but Sir Simon and his two assistants are too tired and weak to get up. Their nerves are completely shattered. They sit up and peer around fearfully at the slightest noise. The headless skeleton cannot peer, of course, so his bones vibrate instead. At last they decide to give in on one thing — the bloodstain on the library floor....

**Sir Simon**   We won't renew the bloodstain.

**Spirit**   They're simply not worthy of it.

**Headless Skeleton**   And what's more, they just don't deserve it.

**Narrator**   Finally, Sir Simon and his assistants have to rise from their coffins and get back to their haunting — they are still dedicated to their jobs. However, they take care to move around quietly. Sir Simon has stolen the bottle of Rising Sun Lubricator from Mr Otis's bedroom and is keeping his chains well oiled.

   Despite these precautions, the twins have struck again and again. Strings have been stretched across the corridor to trip the ghosts in the dark. On one occasion, with Sir Simon dressed for the part of 'Black Baxter' or 'The Huntsman of Hogley Woods', he has met with a severe fall — caused by banana skins spread by the twins down the oak staircase. Furious, Sir Simon has decided to make one final effort....

**Sir Simon**   (*dressing in ghastly garb*) Prepare yourselves for the final haunting! You will notice that I am donning the devastating disguise of 'Reckless Rupert', also known as 'The Double-headed Earl'.

**Spirit**   (*admiringly*) Frightfully good!

**Headless Skeleton**   One head gibbers madly while the other head screams insanely. I like it.

**Sir Simon**   Then, forward to victory!

   (*They rush through the walls of the castle and materialize outside the twins' room. The door is ajar.*)

**Sir Simon** (*whispering*) I will enter first with both my heads revolving while both of you wave your phosphorescent limbs around. Ready? Go!

**Narrator** He steps forward, flinging the door wide to achieve an impressive entrance — and receives the contents of an enormous jug of water that had been balanced above the door!

**Sir Simon** (*chilled to the bone*) AAAAAaaaaahhhhhhBBBBBrrrrrrr!

**Headless Skeleton** (*shocked to the core*) I can hear those evil-minded twins laughing their heads off in their room.

**Spirit** (*moaning*) Woe is us! Quick, we must get Sir Simon back to his lead coffin before he catches his death of cold.

**Narrator** Back at the coffins, the three of them give up all hope of overcoming the Otis family. They sink into despair.

*SCENE 8   The long, dusty corridors of the castle.*

**Narrator** In a well-concealed corner (to escape the notice of the twins) Sir Simon is sitting alone. He is weeping and holding his head in his hands. At this embarrassing moment, Virginia, who is walking along the corridor, hears the weeping and peers into the corner.

**Virginia** (*amazed*) It's the Canterville Ghost!

**Sir Simon** (*preparing to vanish*) Oh ...

**Virginia** (*hastily*) No, don't go.

**Sir Simon** But your horrible brothers ...

**Virginia** They will be off to school tomorrow. So, after that — if you behave yourself — no one will annoy you.

**Sir Simon** (*shaking his head*) It is absurd asking me to behave myself. Quite absurd. I must rattle my chains, and groan through keyholes, and walk about at night, if that is what you mean. It is my only reason for existing.

**Virginia**  It is no reason at all for existing, and you know you have been very wicked. Mrs Umney told us the first day we arrived here, that you had killed your wife.

**Sir Simon**  Well, I quite admit it, but it was purely a family matter, and concerned no one else.

**Virginia**  It is very wrong to kill any one.

**Sir Simon**  (*annoyed*) You have to understand the background. You have to know something about my wife herself, a bullying, terrifying monster of a woman. No man in his right mind would have married her. I had no choice in the matter. My father forced me into my marriage with Lady Eleanore. It was for family prestige, you know. What a soul-destroying woman. I still wince when I walk past her picture in the library. Did you know that my friend William Shakespeare got his ideas for his play, *The Taming of the Shrew*, from my scolding, nagging wife, Lady Eleanore de Canterville?

**Virginia**  No, I didn't. But I still say what you did was very wrong.

**Sir Simon**  But I haven't finished yet. She nagged and bullied me day after day, year after year. She abused my friends with her lashing tongue until I had no friends left. She even stopped me from practising with my ninepins. With her ceaseless bullying she destroyed my very soul. Finally I could take no more. (*He pauses.*) However, it is no matter, for it is all over, and I don't think it was very nice of her brothers when they caught me, after nine years' searching, to starve me to death in this very castle, even though I did kill her.

**Virginia**  Starve you to death? Oh, Mr Ghost, I mean Sir Simon, are you hungry? I'll get you a sandwich.

**Sir Simon**  No, thank you, I never eat anything now; but it is very kind of you, all the same, and you are much nicer than the rest of your horrid, rude, vulgar, dishonest family.

**Virginia**  (*stamping her foot*) Stop! It is you who are rude, and horrid, and vulgar; and as for dishonesty, you know you stole the paint out of my paint-box to try and touch up that ridiculous bloodstain in the library. First you took all my reds, including the vermilion, and I couldn't do any more sunsets, then you took the emerald green and the chrome-yellow, and finally I had nothing left but indigo and Chinese white, and could only do moonlight scenes, which are always depressing to look at, and not at all easy to paint. I never told on you, though I was very annoyed, and it was ridiculous. Whoever heard of emerald-green blood?

**Sir Simon** (*meekly*) Well, really, what was I to do? It's a very difficult thing to get real blood these days and, as your brother started it all with his Paragon Detergent, I saw no reason why I shouldn't have your paints. As for colour, that's always a matter of taste.

**Virginia** The best thing you can do is to emigrate to America. My father will be only too happy to give you a free ticket, and though there's a heavy duty on spirits of every kind, there'll be no difficulty about getting you through customs. Once in New York, you are sure to be a great success. I know lots of people who'd give thousands of dollars to have a family ghost.

**Sir Simon** I don't think I'd like America.

**Virginia** (*annoyed*) Well, good evening! I'll go and ask papa to get the twins an extra week's holiday.

**Sir Simon** Please don't go, Miss Virginia. I am so lonely and so unhappy, and I really don't know what to do. I want to go to sleep and I cannot.

**Virginia**   That's quite absurd! You just have to go to bed and blow out the candle. It's very difficult sometimes to keep awake, especially at church, but there's no difficulty at all about sleeping. Why, even babies know how to do that, and they're not very clever.

**Sir Simon**   I have not slept for three hundred years, for three hundred years I have not slept and I am so tired. Yes, death must be so beautiful. To lie in the soft brown earth, with the grasses waving above your head, and listen to *silence*. To have no yesterday, and no tomorrow. To forget time, to forgive life, to be at peace.

**Virginia**   Poor, poor ghost . . .

**Sir Simon**   But before I can have my resting-place in the pinewoods yonder, the Canterville Legend must be fulfilled. You see, as a punishment for my crime, my spirit is destined to haunt Canterville Castle. Only the Canterville Legend has the power to break this curse.

**Virginia**   What is the Canterville Legend?

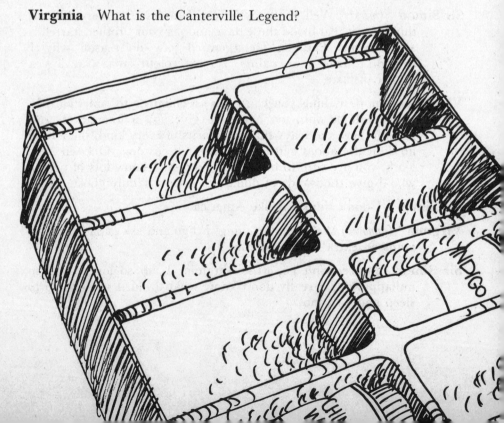

**Sir Simon**  Have you ever read the old prophecy painted on the library window?

**Virginia**  Oh, often. I know it quite well. It's painted in curious black letters, and it's difficult to read. There are only six lines. (*She recites them.*)

> When a golden girl can win
> Prayer from the lips of sin,
> When the barren almond bears,
> And a little child gives away its tears,
> Then shall all the house be still
> And peace come to Canterville.

But I don't know what they mean.

**Sir Simon**  They mean that you must weep for me — for my terrible sin — because I have no tears; and pray with me for my soul, because I have no faith. Then the Angel of Death will have mercy on me.

**Virginia**  I'm not afraid to do that, and I will ask God to have mercy on you.

**Sir Simon**  (*joyfully*) I am to find rest at last.

**Narrator**  Sir Simon and the golden-haired Virginia kneel and pray together for the peace of Sir Simon's soul. Then Sir Simon rises and kisses Virginia's hand. Virginia weeps as, very slowly, Sir Simon fades away. Finally, he is gone forever from Canterville Castle.... Suddenly, all the other members of the Otis family rush down the corridor.

**Mr Otis**  Great heavens, Virginia. Where have you been? We've been searching the castle and the grounds for you. Your mother has been frightened to death. You must never play these practical jokes any more.

**Stars and Stripes**  Except on the Ghost! Except on the Ghost!

**Mrs Otis**  (*kissing Virginia and smoothing her hair*) My own darling, thank goodness you are found. You must never wander off like this again.

**Virginia**   I have been talking to the Ghost. He's dead now. He had been very wicked, but he was really sorry for all that he had done.

**Mr Otis**   (*looking out the window*) Look! (*They all go to the window, except Virginia.*) The old withered almond tree has blossomed. I can see the flowers quite plainly in the moonlight. It's a miracle!

**Virginia**   God has forgiven him. He can rest in peace.

*CURTAIN*

## Questions

1   Why is Scene 1 important to the play?

2   How are tension and suspense built up in Scene 2?

3   How does the Otis family triumph over Sir Simon and his assistants in Scene 3?

4   In what way is Scene 4 an amusing scene?

**5**  What results flow from the celebrated peal of demoniac laughter given by Sir Simon in the middle of Scene 5?

**6**  In Scene 6, Sir Simon and his assistants have prepared ghastly haunting experiences for the Otis family. Fill in the following table by showing the ghastly haunting experience(s) prepared for each family member. Note the example.

| Washington | (a) clutch of a bony hand<br>(b)<br>(c)<br>(d) |
|---|---|
| Mrs Otis | (e) |
| Mr Otis | (f) |
| Virginia | (g)<br>(h) |
| Twins | (i)<br>(j)<br>(k)<br>(l) |

**7**  What terrible trick is played on Sir Simon in Scene 7?

**8**  What other side of Sir Simon's character is presented to us in the last scene? Does this other side of his character make us feel sympathy for him? Why or why not?

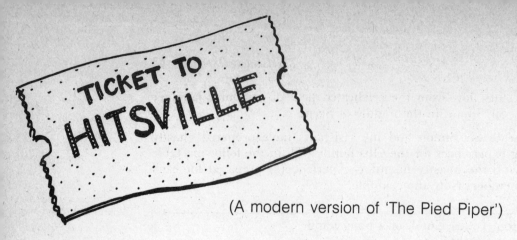

# TICKET TO HITSVILLE

(A modern version of 'The Pied Piper')

## Bill Tordoff and David Doughan

### Cast

Ed Piper
The Mayor
7 Mothers
2 Fathers
4 Councillors
5 Rats *(A pop group)*
10 Kids
Voice

## SCENE I

*A street.*

**Mother 1**  (*offstage*) Charlton! Charlton! (*She enters in a rage.*) Charlton! Charlton!

**Mother 2**  (*offstage*) Lester! Lester! (*She enters, also in a rage.*) Lester!

**Mother 1**  Have you lost your Lester?

**Mother 2**  I have. I can't find him anywhere.

**Mother 1**  Same with our Charlton. Let me know if you find him, will you?

**Mother 2**  Of course I will, but I've looked everywhere. I just can't think where he can be.

**Mother 1**  They can't be far away in a town this size. Let's shout again. Charlton!

**Mother 2**  Lester!

**Both**  Charlton! Lester!

(*Enter **Mothers 3**, **4** and **5** with shopping bags.*)

**Mother 5**  (*to* **Mother 1**) Here! Are you looking for your Charlton?

**Mother 1**  Yes, I am.

**Mother 3**  Oh, I thought you were both tuning up for a cuptie.

**Mother 5**  Oh, be quiet, Janet.

**Mother 1**  Have *you* seen him?

**Mother 5**  Yes, we saw him just now (*to* **Mother 2**) with your Lester.

**Mother 1**  Where did you see them?

**Mother 2**  I've looked all over.

**Mother 5**  Well, we were coming from the shops, you see ...

**Mother 3**  There was this lovely young man in the greengrocer's and he gave me this look ...

**Mother 5**  Oh, shut up a minute, Janet. We were going past that dance-hall place in Mill Street. What do they call it?

**Mother 1**  Not the Cavern?

**Mother 5**  That's right, the Cavern.

**Mother 4**  And there were your Charlton, and your Lester, and Mrs Roebottom's Roger just going in.

**Mother 1**  They never were! The young devil! How many times has he been told never to go near that Cavern?

**Mother 2**  Wait till their fathers come home.

(*Enter* **Mother 6**.)

**Mother 4**  Oh, Mrs Roebottom, are you looking for Roger by any chance?

**Mother 6**  Yes, I am. Have any of you seen him?

**Mother 5**  Yes, we've seen him all right. Going into that Cavern.

**Mother 6**  Oh, that Cavern! Not my Roger!

**Mother 2**  To hear those Rats, I suppose.

**Mother 3**  Those what?

**Mother 5**   Don't you know anything, Janet? You must have heard of the Rats?

**Mother 1**   This jazz band.

**Mother 2**   Pop group.

**Mother 1**   It's all the same.

**Mother 6**   All long hair.

**Mother 5**   Never wash their necks.

**Mother 4**   Carrying on!

**Mother 2**   Disgusting!

**Mother 6**   They are. And it's disgusting the effect they're having on the young people in this district.

**Mother 1**   You can never find your kids when you want them.

**Mother 2**   And there's been too many funny things happening since they came. Things missing.

**Mother 4**   You're right! Only yesterday I put a pie out to cool; a lovely pie it was. I turned my back for five minutes and there it was — gone!

**Mother 6**   And they've a terrible reputation with the tradespeople.

**Mother 3**   Yes, that lovely young man in the greengrocer's was saying. . . .

**Mother 5**   Oh, don't go on about him, Janet!

**Mother 6**   And the noise they make!

**Mother 4**   Music!

**Mother 5**   So-called.

**Mother 6**   All night.

**Mother 3**   All night?

**Mother 6**   Oh yes, the Cavern never closes.

**Mother 2**   And motorbikes.

**Mother 4**   And singing.

**Mother 5**   So-called!

**Mother 1**   The people nearby can't sleep at nights.

**Mother 2**   It's utterly downright disgusting.

**Mother 6**   We shouldn't endure it any longer.

**All**   Hear! Hear!

(*Pause.*)

**Mother 3**   Well, can't anybody do anything about it?

**Mother 6**   It's obvious that somebody should.

**Mother 5**   That's right — but who?

(*They all ponder.*)

**Mother 3**   Well, the council, I suppose — it's their job.

(*Groans.*)

**Mother 5**   Don't be stupid, Janet. When did the council last do anything?

**Mother 1**   Except fill their own pockets.

**Mother 2**   No, it's no use expecting *them* to do anything.

(*Enter **Fathers 1** and **2**.*)

**Father 1**   Hello, Doris, love. Is tea ready?

**Mother 1**   Is tea ready! Of course it's not ready. Do you think I've nothing better to do all afternoon than make your tea? Honestly, sometimes I think you wanted to marry a slave with six pairs of hands. You'll have to wait for it.

**Father 1**   All right, all right, I only asked. Just tell young Charlton to go down to the shop and get me half an ounce of tobacco.

**Mother 1**   You'll have to go yourself: he's not around.

**Father 1**   Well, where is he then?

**Mother 4**   Gone to see the Rats.

**Father 1**   He's what? That long-haired lot? Oo, wait till he gets home.

**Mother 4**   (*to Father 2*) And your Lester was with him.

**Father 2**   Our Lester! When he gets back I'll thrash him within an inch of his life.

**Father 1**   And our Charlton's going to get a real hiding as well.

**Mother 6**   Oh, it's good to see a couple of fathers nowadays who really care for their children.

**Mother 1**   You gave him a real hiding last time, and it didn't work, did it?

**Father 1**   No, but it cheered me up.

**Father 2**   You can't get it into their heads and you can't get it into the other end either.

**Father 1**   Well, something's got to be done. We can't let these Rats bring our kids up for us.

**Father 2**   No, we can't. We've got to get the council on to this.

**Mother 3**   That's just what I said.

**Mother 5**   But the council never do anything about anything.

**Mother 4**   They just don't care.

**Father 2**   True enough. Only the other day I met Councillor Gummersidge in the street and I asked him right out: 'What are you going to do about these Rats?' I said. And he just laughed. Laughed in my face.

**Mothers**   Oo!

**Mother 3**   Oo, it isn't right.

**Father 2**   'What about the Rats?' he says. 'I've no trouble with them,' he says. 'They don't bother me. Why should I do anything?'

**Mother 2**   Scandalous!

**Mother 5**   Typical!

**Father 1**   Well, if they won't do anything on their own, we'll have to *make* them do something.

**Mother 6**   What we need is a deputation.

**Mother 4**   Quite right, we do.

**All**   Hear! Hear!

**Mother 3**   What's one of them?

**Mother 4**   A deputation? Well, it's, er . . .

**Mother 6**   A deputation means that a group of us will have to put this matter to the council. Cogently.

**Father 1**   Er . . . Yes.

**Mother 5**   Right enough!

**Mother 4**   Good idea.

**Mother 2**   That's the stuff.

**Father 2**   Well, there's no time like the present. Let's stir them up, eh? Come on, if you're coming. Out with the Rats!

**Father 1**
**Father 2**   } Out with the Rats!

**All**   Out with the Rats! Out with the Rats!

(*Exeunt chanting, to the tune of 'When the Saints Go Marching In'.*)


## SCENE 2

*The Council Chamber. The* **Mayor** *is asleep and snoring,* **Councillor 1** *is practising putting, and* **Councillors 2, 3** *and* **4** *are playing cards.*

**Voice offstage**   Where's the mayor? I want to see the mayor! I've got to see him. Where is he? I've got to see him.

**Councillor 2**   Who's that?

**Councillor 3**   Sounds like one of Arthur's fan-club. (**Councillors** *laugh.*) Wake him up.

**Councillor 2** (*shaking the* **Mayor**) Arthur, somebody wants you. Sounds like a friend of yours.

**Mayor** What?

**Voice** I've got to see the mayor!

**Mayor** Go and get rid of him, the fool.

**Councillor 1** (*at door*) What's all this noise?

**Voice** Oh, can I see the mayor, please? It's very important. He promised to help my family three years ago and he's done nothing, nothing at all.

**Councillor 1** Have you any money?

(**Councillors** *sit up and listen.*)

**Voice** No.

(**Councillors** *groan and relax.*)

**Councillor 1** Well, if you think his worship the mayor is going to interrupt an important council meeting to deal with a pauper, you're mistaken. Come back next year. (*They laugh.*)

**Councillor 2** All alike. They think we've nothing better to do than run their errands for them.

**Councillor 3** Why isn't he at work, in any case? It's a working day.

**Mayor** Some of these so called working-classes wouldn't know work if they saw it.

**Councillor 1** Bone idle.

**Councillor 2** All alike!

**Councillor 3** Shiftless!

**Councillor 4** Disgusting!

**Councillor 4** I watched a chap outside our house the other day. Supposed to be digging the road up, or something. So, just for interest, I stood at the window and timed him, and in four hours he rested for twenty minutes! I'd promised Jack here a game of snooker, so I couldn't watch him any longer, but when I came home he'd gone already, just because it was raining a bit.

**Councillor 1**   I hear it flooded some of the cottages at the bottom end.

**Councillor 2**   Yes, it's the only time the floors get washed, by all accounts

(*Laughter.*)

**Councillor 4**   I suppose they'll be up here soon, whining about it.

**Councillor 3**   Well, you can't blame them, can you?

**Councillor 4**   Of course I can blame them. I don't ask them to look after my house. Why should I look after theirs?

**Councillor 1**   Anyway, we've more important things in hand. Deal again, Charlie.

(*Noise off: shouts of 'Out with the Rats'.*)

**Mayor**   Now what is it? Go and see who it is.

**Councillor 4**   (*at the window*) Some hooligans shouting outside. I must see the chief constable about the noise. Ey! They're coming here.

**Councillor 3**   They must want to see *us*.

**Councillor 1**   Can't the doorman keep them out?

**Councillor 4**   No: there's too many of them.

**Councillor 3**   We don't want them to see us like this.

(*Cards etc. are cleared away. They sit around the table and look studious. Enter the* **Parents** *chanting and carrying banners.*)

**Mayor**   Yes . . . er . . . well . . . er . . .

**Councillor 2**   That's a very good point.

**Councillor 1**   So we should er . . .

(**Parents** *lean forward to listen.*)

**Councillor 4**   What do you people think you're playing at, disturbing an important council meeting like this? Can't you see how hard we're working? Go on, off with you.

**Mayor**   Yes. The matter in hand. Now . . .

**Father 1**   Shut up and listen to us! We've come here to find out what you lot are going to do about these Rats.

**Mayor**   Rats? I'm not the rat-catcher, my good man.

(*Laughter from* **Councillors**.)

Why not go to him with your little problem?

**Father 1**   Not those rats. The lot at the Cavern.

**Mayor**   I don't understand you.

**Councillor 2**   Your worship may remember that the council rented the property in Mill Street for cultural purposes. It brings in a good rent.

**Mayor**   Ah! The musician laddies!

**Father 2**   Musicians! That's not music. It's rubbish!

**Mother 6**   It's no good pretending the council don't know about this. We all signed a petition last year protesting against the noise.

**Mother 1**   And the thieving.

**Mother 2**   And that Cavern's open till all hours.

**Mother 4**   They're a very bad influence on the kids.

**Father 1**   So what are you going to do?

**Father 2**   Because we're staying here until you do something for a change.

(**Parents** *start singing 'We Shall Not Be Moved'.*)

**Mayor** Steady, steady. You know, this is a knotty problem. It's not as easy as it seems. I'm sure we've done all we can.

**Mother 3** Well, what have you done?

**Mother 5** Go on, tell us.

**Mother 6** What measures have you taken?

**Councillor 1** Well, that's soon answered, isn't it, Joe?

**Councillor 2** Yes, I mean, for a start, we've done . . . er . . . well . . . er . . .

**Councillor 3** We've tried doing . . . well, you know, we've done er . . .

**Father 2** Nothing! You've done nothing!

**Father 1** Not a thing!

**Mother 1** That's right, Albert.

**Mother 2** You haven't raised a fat finger!

**Mother 3** You've never even thought about it, I bet.

**Mother 6** And we're here today to see that you do something, now.

**Mayor** Such as?

**Mother 6** I beg your pardon?

**Mayor** (*standing*) Such as what? You come breaking in here full of ideas. Just what do you suggest that we do? Go on, tell us.

**Father 2** Well, that's easy. I mean, all you have to do is . . . er . . .

**Mother 2** What he means is that you could always try . . . er . . . well . . .

**Mayor** There you are! You've no idea at all! Here we've been racking our brains night and day, us, the cream of the town, and if we can't think of anything I'm sure you can't.

**Mother 3** Well, but I mean, someone's got to do something.

**Councillor 3**  Well, what?

(*Pause.* **Ed Piper** *bursts in.*)

**Ed**  Hello, folks! I gather you have some difficulty? Maybe I can help you? Piper, Ed Piper's the name. You've seen the Ed Piper show on your TV? 'The Ed Piper Cavern TV Spectacular'.

(*Murmurs of recognition.*)

Like groovy, man, groovy! Have a card! Have a card!

(*He distributes cards to all.*)

You see, you're not the first people who've had this kind of trouble; oh, no! Let me guess — it wouldn't be — the Rats! — would it?

(*Nods.*)

I thought so. Well, folks, consider your troubles over as of right now! I'm here. And I can guarantee you 100 per cent success, first time and every time, with my method. I'll get rid of your Rats like immediately, folks. But hey, look, fellers, I don't do it for my health, see? I guess you guys could afford — let's say — £1000?

**Mayor**   £1000! Out of the question!

**Councillor 1**   Ridiculous! (**Councillors** *murmur agreement*.)

**Councillor 2**   Would you take fifty?

**Mayor**   I admit, he may be all right, but ...

**Father 1**   No buts about it! Come on, you can afford it. Anything to get rid of those Rats!

**Mother 1**   And it's not as if you'd done anything. Let him have a try, at least.

**Father 2**   Yes, let him have a go.

**Mother 2**   Yes, give him a chance.

**Mother 3**   You've done nothing.

**Mother 4**  Let him try.

**Mother 5**  See if he can do anything.

**Mother 6**  Give him a chance.

**Mayor**  But, I think we need to know a little more about our friend's methods before we provide £1000 of the ratepayers' hard-earned money.

**Councillor 2**  Hear, hear.

**Ed**  I'm sorry, Mr Mayor. The way I work is my own affair, but I guarantee it's legal. And no results, no fee. You can't lose.

**Mayor**  But, £1000 ...

**Father 1**  Stop butting! Are you a mayor or a billygoat? Look: you lot are public servants, right? (*Nods.*) Well, we're the public — so get serving!

**Father 2**  You do what we say or we'll throw you out and elect a proper council, see? Well?

**Ed**  One moment, folks. Lets get this straight, Mr Mayor. If I rid this town of the Rats, you'll pay me a thousand pounds? Right?

(*The **Mayor** looks round. **Councillors** nod.*)

**Mayor**  Right, we agree.

(*Cheers from **Parents**.*)

**Ed**  Well, gee, thanks, folks — and you won't regret it — because I guarantee — me, Ed Piper in person — I promise you that by this time tomorrow there won't be a single Rat left in this town!

(*More cheers.*)

### SCENE 3

*The Cavern. On stage, the **Rats** are singing and playing. The **Kids** are dancing and screaming. **Ed Piper** sits at a side table. He is wearing dark glasses and has a briefcase. There is also a record-player on stage. When the song ends, applause.*

**Mother 7** *appears in the main doorway at the top of a flight of stairs. She pushes through the crowd to her daughter,* **Kid 4***, who is practising dancing, and pulls her round. The music stops.*

**Mother 7**   What do you think you're doing, staying here till all hours? I'm sick and tired of worrying about you, and when your Dad gets home he's asking where you are and wanting his cigs fetching.

**Kid 4**   Well, I'm sick and tired of fetching cigs for my Dad. He spends half his time telling me not to smoke and the other half telling me to fetch his cigs for him. He can fetch his own.

**Mother 7**   Oh, he's fetched his own, don't you worry, my girl. And then he told me to fetch you home because it's late.

**Kid 4**   It's not late: it's only ten o'clock.

**Mother 7**   *Only* ten o'clock, and you didn't even come home for your tea!

**Kid 4**   Well, why should I? There's nothing to do at home except sit and knit and watch telly and fetch my Dad's cigs. It's dead boring.

**Mother 7**   Boring or not, you're coming home now. Come on.

   (*She drags her daughter towards the exit, while the other* **Kids** *mimic her, laugh, and shout. The* **Rats** *jeer. She turns in the doorway.*)

   You kids'll soon be laughing on the other side of your faces. Listen! There's been a council meeting today, and we've persuaded the council to do something about this place. They've hired a special agent, and he's guaranteed that this place will be closed down in twenty-four hours. (*to the* **Rats**) And you lot'll have gone. So, if you youngsters have any sense you'll go home now. (*to* **Kid 4**) Come on, you!

   (**Mother 7** *and* **Kid 4** *go out. Pause.* **Kids** *look uneasy, look at watches. The* **Rats** *confer together, and as they do, the* **Kids** *gather round them.*)

**Rat 1**   Stupid peasant.

**Rat 2**   Grotty old potwasher. Come on, let's dig that crazy rhythm again.

**Rat 3**   No.

**Rat 2**   What?

**Rat 3**   I got a hunch the old dame's on to something. She's too stupid to make up that sort of story out of her own tiny mind.

**Rat 4**   So?

**Rat 3**   So the snotty old council have hired an agent to kick us out.

**Rat 4**   So what?

**Rat 5**   So what? Remember the jail in the last burg? The police threw every rule in the book at us.

**Rat 3**   Yeah. Besides, I'm bored with this place. Let's move on before things get hot.

**Rat 1**  Aw, I like it here.

**Rat 2**  Me too. Look, they've tried to turn us out before. We can always tip the council some extra lolly. It's probably what they want.

**Rat 3**  I say let's move.

**Rat 1**
**Rat 2**  } Yeah!

**Kid 1**  Don't go!

**Kid 2**  Please, Rats!

**Kid 3**  Stay with us!

**Kid 5**  Stay!

**Kid 6**  Stay!

**All**  Stay! Stay! Stay!

(*They chant and keep on chanting. The* **Rats** *plug their ears but grin and nod to each other.*)

**Rat 1**  (*waving for silence*) OK. We'll stay!

(*The* **Kids** *cheer.* **Ed** *stands and climbs on to the stage.*)

**Ed**  Huh! Stay! Stay! A talented, swingy group like you are going to stay in this dump?

**Kid 10**  It's not a dump.

**Kid 2**  It's a great place!

(*Other* **Kids** *shout agreement.*)

**Kid 3**  It's the best joint in town!

**Ed**  OK. So it's the best in town, but what a town! A one-horse, one-eyed burg that no one ever comes to unless he's lost. Once you've been to the capital, once you've been to Hitsville, you know what a real place is.

**Kid 5**  Who do you think you are?

**Kids**  Yeah!

**Ed**  Who do I think I am? Who do I think I am? If you've not heard of me, this place must be worse than I thought. You must be cuboid, man.

**Kid 6**  I've seen his face somewhere.

**Kid 5**  So have I.

**Kid 7**  On the telly!

**Kid 3**  Yeah, on the box.

**Kid 8**  Yeah, last night.

(**Ed** *removes his glasses.*)

**Kid 9**  It's Ed Piper!

**Kids**  Ed Piper!

**Ed**  Right! You're on the beam! It's Ed himself!

(*He takes cards from his pocket and gives one to **Kid 9**.*)

What's this, eh?

**Kid 9**  'When to scream. When not to scream.'

(*The others gather round.*)

**Kid 5**  When to stare at camera.

**Kid 3**  When to tap knee.

**Kid 7**  When to scream.

**Kid 1**  When to beam.

**Kid 8**  When to clap.

**Kid 10**  When to snap.

**Ed**  Yes! These are audience instruction cards for the Ed Piper show. And on the other side ...

**Kid 9**  It's an admission ticket!

**Ed**  Yes! A free admission ticket for the greatest show of them all! Take one! Read all about it!

(*He scatters tickets. The **Kids** scramble for them. While they read them, **Ed** goes up to the **Rats**.*)

So you're going to stay here! (*He motions at the **Rats'** equipment.*) A group that's got what it takes is going to waste the best years of its life playing with crummy, cheap, sixty-quid guitars and seventy-quid amplifiers. Listen, kids! I've been watching you. I've got plans for you. There's a place for you on the E.P. show! Imagine, kids, imagine, those millions of drooling dollies all over the country seeing you on the box, then belting down to the record bars for your latest disc.

**Rat 1**  Zowee!

**Rat 3**  Aw, gee!

**Ed**  And what will it lead to?

**Rat 2**  More TV shows!

**Ed**  More TV shows.

**Rat 4**  Radio shows!

**Ed**  Radio shows.

**Rat 5**  Continental tours!

**Ed**  Continental tours.

**Rat 1**  American tours!

**Ed**  American tours.

**Rat 2**  Our first film!

**Rat 4**  Knighthoods! (***Rat 3*** *kneels*.)

**Rat 5**  Arise, Sir Rat!

**All Rats**  Aw!!

**Ed**  Right! All these plus a regular spot in the Ed Piper Cavern TV Spectacular.

> 'Each and every Friday night
> Dollies screaming with delight.
> Come to my Ed Piper cave
> To see those chicks who scream and rave.'

**Rat 5**  This sounds great.

**Rat 4**  This sounds *too* great.

**Rat 1**  This sounds phony. (*He gestures to the others and they huddle together*.) You hear what he says?

**Rat 4**  Yeah, we hear what he *says*.

**Rat 2**  But does he mean it?

**Rat 3**  Can he prove it?

**Rat 5**  We need time to think it over.

**Rat 1**  (*crossing to* ***Ed***) We need time to think it over.

**Ed** (*putting his arm round **Rat 1**'s shoulder and returning to the group*) Sorry, kids, time's the one thing I can't give, because to me time is money, big money. I can give you your big chance, I can give you plush spots, golden discs, I can give you the moon and the stars, but I can't give you time. You've got exactly (*consults watch*) one minute to decide. Are you going to rot here all your lives until your hair goes grey and your guitar strings sag and your valves burn out? Or are you going to reach out with both hands and take this golden chance? (*They look undecided.*) Come on, kids. Make the break. You've still time to reach Hitsville tonight.

(*The **Rats** look at each other, still hesitating.*)

Right! I'm off! (*He moves to the door.*)

**Rat 1**  Let's go!

**Rat 2**  Ed!

**Rat 4**  Wait!

**Rat 3**  We're coming!

**Rat 5**  We'll do it!

(*They grab their kit and rush after him. The **Kids** try to block their way, but the **Rats** fight their way through, shouting.*)

**Rats**  We're going! We're off! Goodbye, kids!

**Kids**  Rats! Please! Don't go! Don't leave us! We need you! Please! Please! Rats!

(*They follow the **Rats** out. Noise of motorbikes and **Kids** shouting and howling. Exit **Ed**. Pause. Enter **Mayor** at the other door. He looks round the hall.*)

**Mayor**  (*calling*) They've gone. (*Enter **Councillors**.*)

**Councillor 2**  What?

**Mayor**  The Rats. They've gone.

**Councillor 1**  (*examining the stage*) And gone for good, by the look of it.

**Councillor 3**  But why should they go?

**Councillor 4**   Who cares?

**Mayor**   Right. It's saved us £1000.

(*Re-enter* **Ed**.)

**Councillor 4**   Hello, Mr Piper! Just too late, eh?

**Councillor 2**   Yes, you missed your chance there, Piper.

**Councillor 3**   I wonder why they went so suddenly?

**Councillor 1**   It doesn't matter why they went. They've gone, and that's that.

**Councillor 4**   And it's saved us £1000. (*They start to go.*)

**Ed**   Oh, no, it hasn't — They went because I got rid of them, and I'll have my money now. On the nail. As agreed.

(**Mayor** *and* **Councillors** *laugh.*)

**Mayor**   Don't give us that tale, Piper. They've gone of their own accord, so don't you try and cash in on it. Never mind, I think we can manage £5 travelling expenses, can't we?

**Councillor 3**   Yes, he tried to help.

**Councillor 1**   Rubbish! He's done nothing.

**Councillor 4**   I think £2 is the limit, Arthur.

**Ed**   Two pounds! You promised me a thousand if the Rats went, and you'll give me a thousand or else I'll ...

**Councillor 1**   Or else what? They've gone.

**Councillor 2**   And they'll not come back now.

**Councillor 3**   Hard luck, Mr Piper.

**Ed**   It'll be your hard luck, not mine, if I don't get my money now.

(**Ed** *moves towards the* **Mayor**, *but is tripped up by* **Councillors 1** *and* **2**. *The* **Mayor** *and* **Councillors** *move towards the door.*)

(*yelling*) I'll give you lot a last chance. It might not be only the Rats who'll go ...

**Mayor**  We hope not, because we hope you'll go as well, Mr Piper. (**Councillors** *laugh.*) Well, we've wasted enough time. We've got work to do, if you haven't. Come on, lads.

*(Exeunt. **Ed** follows them to the doorway.)*

**Ed**  I'll get even with you lot! Just you wait!

*(**Ed** stands in the doorway, looks round, then moves to the record-player and puts a record on. A **Kid** looks in, then beckons the others, who all filter in except **Kid 9**. They stand glaring at **Ed**, who switches off the record.)*

**Kid 1**  They've gone.

**Kid 2**  To rotten Hitsville.

**Kid 10**  To be on his show.

**Kid 4**  His grotty show.

**Kid 6**  What are we supposed to do now they've gone?

**Kid 7**  We'll never see them again.

**Kid 8**  Never ever.

**Kid 3**  Never ever ever.

*(Pause.)*

**Kid 5**  It's all Piper's fault.

**Kid 2**  Yeah, stupid Piper.

*(They stare at **Ed**.)*

**Kid 1**  Let's get him.

*(They advance slowly on **Ed**, who retreats.)*

**Ed**  Steady, kids. You *can* see them again.

*(They stop.)*

**Kid 3**  What?

**Ed**  The Rats: you *can* see them again.

**Kid 4**  Yeah, on the telly. Come on, get him, kids.

**Ed**   No! No! You can see them in the flesh! ... Look, what's that in your pocket?

**Kid 4**   Admission tickets!

**Kid 1**   They're no good to us.

**Kid 8**   How would we get there?

**Kid 7**   We're skint.

**Kid 6**   As always.

**Kids**   Yeah!

(*They tear up the tickets.*)

**Kid 1**   Get him!

(*They advance on* **Ed**, *driving him up onto the stage.*)

**Ed**   No, listen, kids. Give me a break!

**Kid 2**   We'll break *you!*

(*They lift him, ready to throw him off the stage.*)

**Ed**   No! No! Stop a bit! (*They stop, but keep him up in the air.*) Put me down a minute, kids.

(*Pause, then slowly they lower him.*)

**Ed**  Listen, kids! You want to go to Hitsville, don't you?

**Kids**  Yeah!

**Ed**  And you want to leave this place for ever, don't you?

**Kids**  Yeah!

**Ed**  Right! I'll pay your fare. (**Kids** *murmur excitedly.*)

**Kid 1**  Why?

**Ed**  Why? Because I need a new, full-time audience on the E.P. show. I'm looking for super-kids who can scream and yell and clap twice as loud as ordinary kids. And I think you're those kids! Come on! Let's practise now! Ready?

**Kids**  Yeah!

**Ed**  All right! Let's go! Follow the cards!

(*Holds up 'applaud' card. They applaud.*)

You call that applause? I can clap louder with one hand. Come on, again.

(*Holds up 'applaud' again, then 'stop'. They stop, but raggedly.*)

'STOP' means dead-stop: from applause to nothing in a micro-second. Try again.

(*They do. This time it's better.*)

Great! Now let's swing it.

(*He holds up 'applaud', 'stop', 'applaud', 'stop', 'laugh', 'stop', 'clap', 'stop', 'scream', 'stop'.*)

That isn't screaming! I want a scream that'll perforate the eardrums of every old square from here to Hitsville. Come on! Again!

(*He holds up 'scream', then, after a long scream, 'stop'.*)

Great, like groovy! Let's go!

(*The **Kids** scream. He goes to the exit holding up 'scream' card. The **Kids** follow him, screaming. Exeunt. Pause. Enter through the other door **Kid 9**, wearing school uniform, carrying satchel, sports bag, hockey bag and violin. Sound of cheering **Kids** and bus moving off.*)

**Kid 9**   So all my friends have gone with Ed
To sing and scream with glee.
While I get left behind at school
To take my GCE.

My Dad says later I'll be glad
I stayed in every night
To do my French and History:
Well, I only hope he's right!

*CURTAIN*

(*As the cast take the curtain-call, **Ed** holds up the 'applaud' card.*)

## Questions

1 What are the feelings of the kids' parents towards the Rats and the Cavern?

2 What are the parents' feelings towards the council and the Councillors?

3 What kind of a person is the Mayor? Give evidence from the play to support your opinion.

4 What kind of people are the Councillors?

5 How does Ed Piper convince the Rats to leave the Cavern and go to Hitsville?

6 What kind of a person is Ed Piper? Give evidence from the play to support your opinion.

7 How do the kids react to the departure of the Rats?

8 How does Ed Piper get the kids to go to Hitsville?

9 Why is Kid 9 left behind?

10 Do you think Ed Piper is justified in wanting to get even with the Mayor and the Councillors? Give a reason for your viewpoint.

11 Do you think that 'Ticket to Hitsville' is a good title for the play? Why or why not?

12 Imagine you are acting in the play. How would you play the part of (a) Ed Piper (b) the Mayor (c) one of the Rats?

13 What criticisms of modern society do you think the playwrights are making?

14 Which character did you like best? Why?

15 Which scene did you like best? Why?

16 Read through the poem 'The Pied Piper of Hamelin' by Robert Browning. Explain how the playwrights have modernized the story.

# THE AFFAIR OF THE LONE BANANA

Spike Milligan
(Script, *The Goon Show*, No. 104)

---

## Cast

Eccles
Inspector Neddie Seagoon
Gravely Headstone
Lady Marks
Mr Henry Crun
Miss Minnie Bannister
Señor Gonzales Mess, né Moriarty
Major Denis Bloodnok
Bluebottle
Cyril Cringinknutt
Fred Nurke
Grytpype-Thynne
Announcer 1
Announcer 2
Additional Voice (A.V.)

---

**FX** = live sound-effects
**GRAMS** = prerecorded effects or music

## Introduction

Fred Nurke is missing! An over-ripe banana in a deserted Cannon Street shipping office is the only clue to his whereabouts. Inspector Ned Seagoon follows the trail to a British Embassy in South America, where he is just in time to help the Embassy staff in a brush with the rebels. Why are Señor Gonzales Mess and his gang trying to cut down the only banana tree in the Embassy gardens? And what is the connection between Fred Nurke and the over-ripe banana in Cannon Street? We shall see ...

**Announcer 1**   This is the BBC Home Service.

**GRAMS**   WAILING.

**Announcer 2**   Yes indeed — to the gay music of Britain's taxpayers, we present the Grune Show.

**ORCHESTRA**   VERY LONG VIGOROUS SYMPHONIC FIN-ISH A LA 'WILLIAM TELL'.

**FX**   EXPLOSION — FALLING GLASS, BITS & PIECES.

**Announcer 1**   And why not?

**Announcer 2**   Yes, why not? Mr Greenslade!

**Announcer 1**   Yes, Master?

**Announcer 2**   Tell the masses what's the play.

**Announcer 1**   Ladies and gentlemen ...

**Announcer 2**   Thank you. Yes, it's ladies and gentlemen in ... 'The Affair of the Lone Banana'!

**ORCHESTRA**   DEEP SINISTER CHORDS HELD UNDER:—

**Announcer 2**   The Affair of the Lone Banana — not a pretty story, I fear; still, the BBC *will* buy this cheap trash. However ... the central character in this story is young Fred Nurke. His father, Lord Marks, made a fortune from the great Marks Laundry business ... but then you've all heard of Laundry Marks ... ha ha ha. But let's start the story from the beginning.

**ORCHESTRA** 'GREENSLEEVES'-TYPE MUSIC ... FLUTE, HARP TO BACKGROUND FOR:—

**Announcer 1** The scene is the country home of the Marks, Matzos Lodge. A mystery has been committed: young Fred Nurke has vanished. Interrogating the residents is a man, tall, dark, handsome, swashbuckling, handsome, intelligent ...

**Eccles** This ain't me, folks — I come in later.

**Announcer 1** No — it's Inspector Neddie Seagoon, late of the eighteenth century and part-inventor of the steam-driven explodable hairless toupée.

**Seagoon** ... Now then my man, your name is — er?

**Headstone** Headstone, Gravely Headstone. My maiden name, you understand.

**Seagoon** I understand. (*aside*) Don't put that down, Sergeant.

**A.V.** Right, sir.

**Seagoon** Headstone, you are a footman.

**Headstone** Two foot six to be exact.

**Seagoon** How lovely to be tall. Headstone, you say Fred Nurke disappeared whilst having a bottle of tea with his mother, Lady Marks.

**Headstone** True — you might say he disappeared from under her very nose.

**Seagoon** What was he doing there?

**Headstone** It was raining, I believe.

**Seagoon** (*self*) Mmm, Lady Marks. (*normal*) Where is her ladyship at the moment?

**Headstone** Me lady hasn't got a ship at the moment.

**Seagoon** I don't wish to know that. Greenslade? Send in Lady Marks or that idiot gardener — he might know something.

**Announcer 1** Right sir. (*calls*) Right, this way you!

**FX** GREAT HEAVY APPROACHING FOOTSTEPS.

**Seagoon**  Ah, Lady Marks, sit down.

**Lady Marks**  Thank you.

**Eccles**  I bet you all thought it was going to be me. Ha hum.

**Seagoon**  Lady Marks — your late husband owned a banana plantation, yes?

**Lady Marks**  In South America.

**Seagoon**  That's abroad, isn't it?

**Lady Marks**  It all depends on where you're standing.

**Seagoon**  Let's put it this way. Is it on the tube?

**Lady Marks**  Silly, silly boy.

**Seagoon**  Please, madam, don't be so evasive. If South America is on the tube — we have ways and means of finding out.

**Lady Marks**  Dear midget, of course it's not on the tube.

**Seagoon**  Now you're talking.

**Lady Marks**  So are you, isn't it fun?

**Seagoon**  Lady Marks — this is a tricky case — I don't think I can —

**Lady Marks**  (*plead*) Inspector, you must find my son — you must — I don't care how much money you spend — in fact, I'll chip in a few bob myself.

**Seagoon**  The offer is tempting. Very well, I accept. Just leave everything to me — your purse, jewels, cheque book, (*fading*) war bonds, trombone . . .

**GRAMS** 'HARRY LIME THEME'.

**Announcer 2**  At the British Passport office in Whitechapel, Seagoon discovered that Fred Nurke had left for Guatemala on a banana boat — disguised as a banana.

**Seagoon**  That's true — I waited for the ship to return but he wasn't on board — he must have got off — at the other side.

**ORCHESTRA & OMNES**  (*Loud applause ... cries of 'Bravo' etc....*)

**Seagoon**  Thank you, thank you — no, don't make it sound rehearsed. My next task was to book a ticket to South America. This I did at a shipping office in Leadenhall Street.

**FX**  SHOP BELL

**Crun**  Mnk — mnk grnk. Who is it? Eh eh? Who is it?

**Seagoon**  Good morning.

**Crun**  Thank you.

**Seagoon**  I want to book to South America.

**Crun**  That's abroad, sir, isn't it?

**Seagoon**  Yes. (*cocky*) It isn't on the tube you know.

**Crun**  Isn't that wonderful — what will they think of next. Ohhh, do sit down, sir.

**Seagoon**  Err — there aren't any chairs.

**Crun**  You can stand up if you wish.

**Seagoon**  Thank you.

**Crun**  No extra charge. Now, let's get some details and documents — we must have documents, you know. I'll just take a few particulars. Now, let's get the details and the documents — we must have documents, you know.

**Seagoon**  Of course.

**Crun**  ... must have documents. Ymnbnkhmn, now, what's all this about? Let me — oh yes. Now, name?

**Seagoon**  Neddie Pugh Seagoon.

**Crun**  (*writing*) N E D D I E ... Neddie — what was next?

**Seagoon**  Neddie *Pugh* Seagoon.

**Crun**  *Pugh*, P H E W.

**Seagoon**  No, it's pronounced Phew but it's spelt P U G H.

**Crun**   Oh, ynmnk, P U G H — there — Neddie Pugh, Seagoon wasn't it?

**Seagoon**   Yes ... S E A G O O N.

**Crun**   Could you spell it?

**Seagoon**   Certainly — S E A G O O N.

**Crun**   Seagoon ... S E A G   er — mnkk — mnkk. (*Goes to sleep.*)

**Seagoon**   G O O N — Seagoon.

**Crun**   O O N — ahhh good, good, good — there, the full name. Now then — address?

**Seagoon**   No fixed abode.

**Crun**   N O ... F I X E D ... A B ... A B —

**Seagoon**   A B O D E.

**Crun**   O D E ... there — no fixed abode — what number?

**Seagoon**   29A.

**Crun**   Twenty nine ... a ... district?

**Seagoon**   London, SW2.

**Crun**   L O N D O N — S O U T H   W E S T ... *Two*, wasn't it?

**Seagoon**   Yes, two.

**Crun**   TW ... It's no good, I'd better get a pencil and paper and write all this down. Minnie ... *Minnie*?? Min, Min, Min, Min, Min, *Minieeeeee*!

**Minnie**   What is it, Henry?

**Crun**   A pencil, please.

**Minnie**   OK buddy.

**Crun**   Minnie, this gentleman is going to South America.

**Minnie**   Ohh — goodbye.

**Crun**   That's where young Fred Nurke went to ...

**Seagoon**  Fred Nurke? That's Fred Nurke's name!

**Crun**  Yes, he went in such a rush he left this behind.

**Seagoon**  Let me see — a banana — a lone banana! So, now my task was easier — I knew that the man I was looking for was one banana short!

**ORCHESTRA**  (*Loud applause ... shouts of 'Bravo' etc....*)

**Announcer 1**  As a tribute to Seagoon's brilliant deductive powers, Max Geldray will now play a loaded sackbut from the kneeling position.

**ORCHESTRA**  MUSIC.

(*Applause.*)

**Announcer 1**  The Affair of the Lone Banana, Chapter Two. With the banana secreted on his person, Neddie Seagoon arrived at the Port of Guatemala where he was accorded the typical Latin welcome to an Englishman.

**Moriarty**  Hands up, you pig swine.

**Seagoon**  Have a care, Latin devil — I am an Englishman. Remember, this rolled umbrella has more uses than one.

**Moriarty**  Oooo!

**Seagoon**  Sorry. Now, what's all this about?

**Moriarty**  It is the revolution — everywhere there is an armed rising.

**Seagoon**  Are you all in it?

**Moriarty**  Right in it — you see, the united anti-socialist neo-democratic pro-fascist communist party are fighting to overthrow the unilateral democratic united partisan bellicose pacifist cobelligerent tory labour liberal party.

**Seagoon**  Whose side are you on?

**Moriarty**  There are no sides — we are all in this together. Now, if you don't mind — we must search you.

**Seagoon**  What for?

**Moriarty**  Bananas. You see, we Guatemalians are trying to over-throw the foreign-dominated banana plantations in this country. Any foreigner found with a banana on him will be shot by a firing squad and asked to leave the country.

**Seagoon**  (*aside*) Curses — I must think quick. Little does he know I suspect him of foul play.

**Moriarty**  Little does he know I've never played with a fowl in my life.

**Seagoon**  Little does he know that he has misconstrued the meaning of the word foul. The word foul in my sentence was spelt F O U L not F O W L as he thought I had spelt it.

**Moriarty**  Little does he know that I overheard his correction of my grammatical error and I am now about to rectify it — aloud. (*Ahem*) So, you suspect me of foul play spelt F O U L and not F O W L.

**Seagoon**  Yes — and you might as well know I'm here to find young Fred Nurke.

**Moriarty**  *That* capitalistic pig! Why, I'll —

**Seagoon**  Don't move, Señor Gonzales Mess, né Moriarty — hands up.

**Moriarty**  Seagoon, put that banana down!

**Seagoon**  And leave myself defenceless?

**Moriarty**  Sapristi Bompet!

**Seagoon**  One step nearer and I fire.

**Moriarty**  Fool — you can't shoot a banana! It's —

**FX**  TWO PISTOL SHOTS.

**Moriarty**  Swine — it was *loaded*!

**Seagoon**  Of course — you don't think I'd threaten you with an unloaded banana? Now come on, tell me — where is Fred Nurke?

**Moriarty**   I will never tell — go on, torture me — smash my skull in — break my bones — put lighted matches in my fingers — tear the flesh from my body, slice lumps off my . . .

**FX**   THUD OF BODY FALLING ON GROUND.

**Moriarty**   Pancho?

**Announcer 2**   Señor?

**Moriarty**   The smelling salts — he's fainted.

**ORCHESTRA**   THEME SPANISH — LIKE DEATH THEME FROM 'CARMEN'. SOFTLY ON TROMBONES WITH TYMPS.

**Announcer 2**   When the Englishman awoke he found himself in a tall dark room with sideboards — it was a prison cell.

**Seagoon**   True, true. The only other occupant was another occupant — apart from that, he was the *only* other occupant. He was chained to the wall by a chain which was attached to the wall — he *appeared* to be a man of breeding and intellect.

**Eccles**   Hello dere.

**Seagoon**   I was wrong. (But wait — could he be Fred Nurke?)

**Eccles**   How's yer old dad, eh?

**Seagoon**   Do you recognise this banana?

**Eccles**   Nope — I don't think I've ever met him before.

**Seagoon**   Then — then are you one banana short?

**Eccles**   Umm, nope — nope, I ain't one short.

**Seagoon**   Curse — then you're *not* Fred Nurke.

**Eccles**   Ohh, ain't I?

**Seagoon**   No.

**Eccles**   Yer mean I'm somebody else?

**Seagoon**   Yes.

**Eccles**  Ooo — who am I?

**Seagoon**  What's your name?

**Eccles**  Eccles.

**Seagoon**  *That's* who you are!

**Eccles**  Oooooooo.

**Seagoon**  There, there, don't take it so hard. Now then, how can I get out of this place?

**Eccles**  Well, there's dat door dere.

**Seagoon**  Right, I'm away! By dawn I'll be safe! Now's the time for *action*! Nothing will stop me now — Farewelllllllll!

**FX**  DOOR OPENS AND CLOSES. TERRIFIC FUSILLADE OF SHOTS, BOMBS, ETC. DOOR OPENS AND CLOSES.

**Seagoon**  It's raining! Is there any other way out of here?

**Eccles**  Would you care to share my supper?

**Seagoon**  Ahh, how about that window up there!

**Eccles**  Oh, you can't eat that.

**Seagoon**  If we could get up to that window.

**Eccles**  Well, get dis iron chain off my neck and I'll help.

**Seagoon**  Right — just put your neck on this block — I'll soon have it off.

**FX**  IRON HAMMER ON ANVIL. THREE HEFTY WHACKS. CHAINS FALL TO FLOOR.

**Seagoon**  There — that's broken it — you're free! How do you feel?

**Eccles**  Don't know — ain't ever had a broken neck before.

**Seagoon**  Come, let's to the task!

**Eccles**  OK.

**FX**  CHAIRS BEING STACKED ONE ON TOP OF THE OTHER. THIS NOISE KEPT GOING IN BACKGROUND.

**Announcer 1**  Ladies and gentlemen, the sound you are hearing is that of Seagoon and Eccles balancing chairs one atop the other. This operation might last some time as they will need to stack at least fifty to a hundred chairs if they are to reach up to the high window. No doubt, after about five minutes, this sound will become very boring — BBC policy therefore decrees that in the interim we entertain you with songs from that well known tenor and market gardener — Mr Cyril Cringinknutt.

**Cringinknutt**  Thankin' yew — Rinky Fulton. My first number tonight I will sing for money — that lovely Yock melody from my latest record which I have just recorded. It's called 'Three Goons in a Fountain' — my melody please, Fred —

**PIANO** ARPEGGIO.

**Cringinknutt**  (*croon*) Three Goons in a fountain — which one will the fountain drown — I got a shop full of Schmutters — I got —

**Announcer 1**  Thank you. Ladies and gentlemen — Seagoon and Eccles have reached the high window so we won't need Cyril Cringinknutt any more, so we'll say —

**FX** ALL THE CHAIRS COLLAPSE — TERRIFIC CRASH. START STACKING THEM UP AGAIN.

**Cringinknutt**  Three Goons in a fountain, which one will the foun —

**FX** DOOR BURSTS OPEN.

**A.V.**  Eyes front — everyone back to their own beds. There is an English gentleman to see you.

**ORCHESTRA** BLOODNOK MARCH.

**Bloodnok**  Aeiough. Bleiough. Arangahahhh. Kitna Budgy Hai. Aeiough and other naughty noises. Now — which one of you two is Eccles and Seagoon?

**Seagoon**  I'm Seagoon except for Eccles.

**Eccles**  I'm Eccles except for Seagoon.

**Bloodnok**  So, you're both Eccles and Seagoon except for each other!

**Seagoon** Yes.

**Bloodnok** I knew I'd get it out of you. I'm the British Chargé d'Affaires — Major Bloodnok, late of Zsa Zsa Gabor's Third Regular Husbands. I've managed to secure your release. I completely overcame the prison guards.

**Seagoon** What with?

**Bloodnok** Money — aeiough — now, everybody onto this ten-seater horse. Nowwww, gid up there.

**FX** GALLOPING HOOVES START AND STOP AT ONCE.

**Bloodnok** Woah. Here we are. The Embassy.

**FX** KNOCK ON DOOR. DOOR OPENS.

**A.V.** Oh, it's you, sir — am I glad you came back. The rebels have been trying to chop down the banana tree in the garden.

**Bloodnok** Dogs! Stand back. (*shouts*) You Latin devils — begone, or by the great artificial paste earrings of Lady Barnett I'll come out there and cut you down — now get out, you Latin devils!

**A.V.** They all went about three hours ago.

**Bloodnok** Never mind. That didn't stop me.

**Seagoon** Gad, Bloodnok, I admire your guts.

**Bloodnok** Why, are they showing?

**Seagoon** Bloodnok, I seek Fred Nurke.

**Bloodnok** He's here to save the British banana industry. In fact, he went out alone, by himself, to dynamite the rebel HQ.

**Seagoon** Then all we can do is wait.

**Bloodnok** Yes — Ellington? Play that mad banjo, man.

**A.V.** Here goes then —

**QUARTET** MUSIC.

(*Applause.*)

**GRAMS** 'HARRY LIME THEME'.

**Announcer 2**   The Affair of the Lone Banana, Chapter Three. In the grounds of the British Embassy our heroes are dug in around the lone banana tree — the last symbol of waning British prestige in South America. They all anxiously await the return of Fred Nurke. Around them, the jungle night is alive with revels — and nocturnal sounds — rain in places, fog patches on the coast. Arsenal 2 — Chinese Wanderers 600.

**FX**   BRAZILIAN JUNGLE AT NIGHT — CRICKETS — AMAZON OWLS — CHIKIKIS AND OTHER NIGHT ANIMALS.

**Seagoon**   Gad, Bloodnok — this waiting is killing me.

**Bloodnok**   Shhhh — not so loud, you fool — remember, even people have ears.

**Seagoon**   Sorry, Major, but my nerves are strung up to breaking point.

**FX**   ONE STRING FIDDLE. DOINGGGGG. SNAP. (QUICK)

**Seagoon**   There goes one now. It's this darkness! You can't see a *thing*!

**Bloodnok**   I know — for three hours now I've been straining my eyes and I've only managed *one* page of the *Awful Disclosures of Maurice Monk*. Four rupees, in a plain wrapper.

**FX**   LONE CRICKET CHIRPING.

**Bloodnok**   Listen — what's making that noise?

**Seagoon**   Cricket.

**Bloodnok**   How can they see to bat in *this* light?

**Eccles**   Major, a man's just climbed over the garden wall.

**Bloodnok**   A boundary! (*aloud*) Well played, sir!

**Seagoon**   Shh, Bloodnok, you fool — that's no cricketer — he's possibly a rebel assassin.

**Bloodnok**   Then one of us must volunteer to go out and get him.

**Seagoon**   Yes — one of us must volunteer.

**Eccles**  Yer, one of us *must* volunteer!

**All**  England for ever!

**ORCHESTRA**  FANFARE MILITAIRE.

**Announcer 1**  The Affair of the Lone Banana, Chapter Four.

**Bloodnok**  One of us *must* volunteer.

**Seagoon**  Yes, one of us must.

**Eccles**  Yup, one of us must.

**Bloodnok**  Well, who's it going to be? Seagoon?

**Seagoon**  I'm sorry — but I have a wife and sixty-three children.

**Bloodnok**  I too have a wife and children. That only leaves dear old —

**FX**  PANICKY RATTLING OF TELEPHONE.

**Eccles**  Hello, hello, operator? Get me the marriage bureau.

**Bloodnok**  Eccles, you coward. Seagoon? You're youngest, you go.

**Seagoon**  Me? You wouldn't send an old man out there!

**Bloodnok**  You're not an old man.

**Seagoon**  Give me five minutes to make up and you'll never know the difference.

**Bloodnok**  Flatten me Cronkler with Spinachmallets. So, *both* of you have turned cowards. That only leaves *me*. Two cowards, and *me*. You know what this means?

**Seagoon**  *Three* cowards.

**Bloodnok**  . . . in a fountain . . . Let's face it — we've all *turned yellow*.

**A.V.**  You speak for yourselves.

**Bloodnok**  (*apologetic*) Ohh, I'm sorry, Ellington, no offence. I know you Irishmen are very brave.

**FX**  PHONE RINGS.

**Bloodnok**  Aeiough. Don't answer that phone unless it's for me.

**Seagoon**  Right. Are you ringing for Major Bloodnok?

**Moriarty**  (*distort*) Yes.

**Seagoon**  It's for you.

**Bloodnok**  Ohhh.

**FX**  RECEIVER OFF HOOK.

**Bloodnok**  Hello? What??? Never — never, d'yer hear me? Never.

**FX**  RECEIVER SLAMMED DOWN.

**Bloodnok**  It was the rebel leader — Gonzales Mess, né Moriarty, he says unless we chop down our banana tree and hand it over to them — we'll die tonight.

**Eccles**  Tonight? Why, that's tonight.

**Bloodnok**  So it is. Fancy him thinking *I'd* chop down the banana to save my lousy skin — ha! ha!

**FX**  HURRIED CHOPPING-DOWN OF TREE.

**Seagoon**  Bloodnok! Put down that forty-ton chopper!

**Bloodnok**  I'm sorry, I picked it up in a moment of weakness.

**Seagoon**  Disgraceful! Chopping down the British banana tree!

**Eccles**  Yer, disgraceful.

**FX**  HURRIED SAWING OF TREE.

**Seagoon**  Eccles! Stop that! Where did you get that saw?

**Eccles**  (*big joke*) From the sea — it's a sea-saw. Ha ha.

**Seagoon**  Silence! We've got to pull ourselves together — this banana tree is the *last one* in South America under British control!

**Bloodnok**  Yes, you're right! We must defend it, with your lives.

**Seagoon**  Remember, lads — somewhere out there, Fred Nurke is working to destroy the rebel HQ — now, throw that chopper and saw over the wall.

**Both**  OK. (*grunt*)

**Seagoon**  Good — now I'm —

**FX**  CLANG AND THUD AS CHOPPER CLOUTS MAN ON NUT.

**Bluebottle**  (*off*) Ohhhhh — my nut — ohh — I have been hitted on my bonce — oh, I have been nutted — I was kipping on the grass and suddenly — *thud*! Oooooh! (Clutches lump on crust.)

**Seagoon**  Come out from behind that wall or I'll throw this at you.

**Eccles**  Put me down!

**Bluebottle**  (*sad*) Enter Bluebottle wearing crash helmet — pauses for audience applause — not a sausage! (Thinks of rude sailor word.)

**Seagoon**  Who is this gallant little knight with unlaced LCC plimsolls?

**Bluebottle**  Who am *I*? I'm the one wot copped that dirty big saw on the nut. (Points to lump area.)

**Seagoon**  Tell me, little jam-stained hero; do you know this jungle well?

**Bluebottle**  Yes — I know the jungule — Tarzan Bluebottle, they call me. (Lifts up sports shirt, shows well-developed ribs and bones. Fills chest with air (*breathe*) — feels giddy so puts on cardboard loin cloth for support.)

**Seagoon**  Could you lead me to the rebel HQ?

**Bluebottle**  (*intimate*) I can show you the very spot.

**Seagoon**  (*intimate*) Where?

**Bluebottle**  (*declaim*) Where that dirty big saw hitted my nut! You rotten nut-hitting swine you! (Does body racked with sobs pose — as done by Robert Newton after seeing income-tax returns.)

**Seagoon**  Right. Eccles, you come with us. Bloodnok — you stay here. Bluebottle — lead on!

**Bluebottle**  Forward! Pulls hat well down over eyes (but pulls it up as cannot see where I'm going). Come, follow me — I —

**FX**  TERRIFYING ROAR OF SAVAGE LION.

**Bluebottle**   Heu heu hu — what was that, my capatain?

**Seagoon**   A man-eating tiger.

**Bluebottle**   Tiger?

**Seagoon**   Yes.

**FX**   WHOOSH.

**Bluebottle**   (*right off*) I do not like this game — I'm going home — I just remembered it's my turn in the barrel — exits left to East Finchley on Council dust cart.

**Seagoon**   Very well, I'll go ahead myself — first I'll disguise myself as a Mexican peon — they'll never recognise me!

**Announcer 1**   The Affair of the Lone Banana, Chapter Five.

**Moriarty**   Signor Grytpype-Thynne — we found this idiot hiding in a dustbin disguised as a Mexican peon.

**Grytpype-Thynne**   Ahhhh — a midget, eh?

**Seagoon**   Have a care.

**Grytpype-Thynne**   No thanks, I don't smoke — sit on a chair.

**Seagoon**   I'll stand.

**Grytpype-Thynne**   Very well, stand on a chair then.

**Seagoon**   So — you're the leader of the rebels?

**Grytpype-Thynne**   Yes. Now — *who are you?*

**Seagoon**   *I won't talk!* Never!

**Grytpype-Thynne**   (*calls off*) The branding irons!

**Seagoon**   I'm Needie Seagoon.

**Grytpype-Thynne**   Oh? Where's Fred Nurke?

**Seagoon**   I don't know.

**Grytpype-Thynne**   So *that's* where he is. Right, Moriarty? We'll go at once to the Embassy — and bring back their banana tree.

**Seagoon**   You won't succeed — it's guarded by Major Dennis Blood-nok.

**Grytpype-Thynne**   Bloodnok? Moriarty — bring money. Seagoon, we'll lock you in here — goodbye.

**FX**   DOOR LOCKS — KEY.

**Seagoon**   Poor fools — the moment they step out — Fred Nurke will get them — they go to their doom!

**FX**   PHONE RINGS — RECEIVER OFF HOOK.

**Seagoon**   Hello?

**Fred Nurke**   (*distort*) Is that the rebel HQ?

**Seagoon**   Yes, but I'm —

**Fred Nurke**   Right, you swines — this is Fred Nurke, and this is my bonanza night — in three seconds a time-bomb explodes in your room, ha ha!

**FX**   CLICK.

**Seagoon**   Three seconds — I've got to get...

**FX**   FOOTSTEPS RUNNING FOR DOOR.

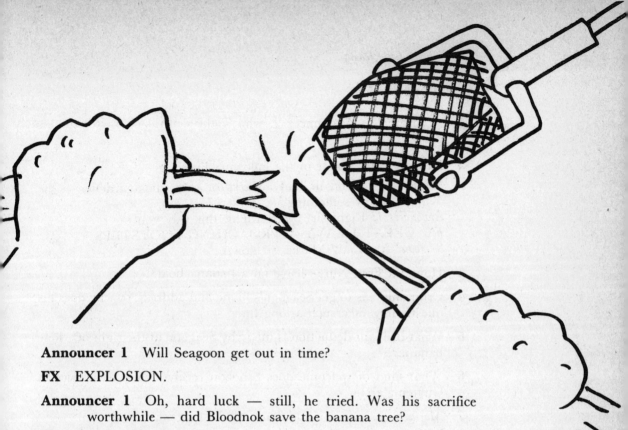

**Announcer 1**  Will Seagoon get out in time?

**FX**  EXPLOSION.

**Announcer 1**  Oh, hard luck — still, he tried. Was his sacrifice worthwhile — did Bloodnok save the banana tree?

**FX**  TREE CRACKING.

**Bloodnok**  Timber!!!

**FX**  TREE CRASHING.

**ORCHESTRA**  SIGNATURE TUNE: UP AND DOWN FOR:—

**Announcer 1**  That was The Goon Show — a recorded programme featuring Peter Sellers, Harry Secombe and Spike Milligan with the Ray Ellington Quartet and Max Geldray. The Orchestra was conducted by Wally Stott. Script by Spike Milligan. Announcer: Wallace Greenslade. The programme produced by Peter Eton.

**ORCHESTRA**  SIGNATURE TUNE UP TO END.

(*Applause.*)

**ORCHESTRA**  'CRAZY RHYTHM' PLAYOUT.

## Questions

1   According to Announcer 2, who is the central character in this play?

2   Explain the humour in the following lines.

*Seagoon:* ... Send in Lady Marks or that idiot gardener — he might know something.
*Announcer 1:* Right sir. (*calls*) Right, this way you!
*FX:* GREAT HEAVY APPROACHING FOOTSTEPS.
*Seagoon:* Ah, Lady Marks, sit down.

3   How did Fred Nurke leave on a banana boat?

4   Crun only has to get Seagoon's name and address, so why does his questioning take such a long time?

5   What brilliant deduction is made by Seagoon at the sight of a lone banana?

6   What kind of welcome does Seagoon receive when he arrives in Guatemala?

7   *Moriarty:* ... Now, if you don't mind — we must seach you.
Why does Seagoon have to be searched?

8   *Seagoon:* ... Little does he know I suspect him of foul play.
*Moriarty:* Little does he know I've never played with a fowl in my life.
Explain the pun (play on words) in these lines.

9   Whom does Seagoon meet in the prison cell?

10   How is the audience entertained while chairs are being stacked up to the prison window?

11   How are Seagoon and Eccles rescued from jail?

12   What happens to Seagoon's nerves as he crouches by the lone banana tree?

13   *Bloodnok:* Listen — what's making that noise?
*Seagoon:* Cricket.
What does Seagoon mean by this? What joke is made on the word?

**14**   How does Seagoon get out of volunteering to find the rebel?

**15**   How does Eccles try to get out of volunteering?

**16**   Both Bloodnok and Eccles try to get rid of the banana tree. How do they go about it?

**17**   What happens as this *Goon Show* ends?

**18**   These shows are famous for the many weird sounds that are used. In your opinion, why are such sounds used?

# THE GHOST OF MUDDLEDUMP MANOR!

Alan Rowe

| Cast |
|---|
| **Compere** |
| **Sir Henry Thorndike** |
| **Reginald,** *his son (or* **Cynthia***, his daughter)* |
| **Charles Muggins,** *a Lancashire nephew* |
| **Sam Billings** (*or* **Sarah Billings**), *a Lancashire neighbour* |
| **Milkman** |

## SCENE

*A lounge room at Muddledump Manor, England. Cast should use English voices. Torches should be used by each member of the cast. It will be possible, this way, to read the sketch and also create an eerie atmosphere. Ghostly music will help. As curtain opens stage is in darkness with each member of the cast shining torch into his/her own face to create spooky effect.*

**Compere**  Ladies and gentlemen, we now cross to Muddledump Manor in England, where we find Sir Henry Thorndike, and his brave band of ghost hunters, waiting to solve the mystery of the family ghost. Strange noises have been heard just after midnight for the past week, and Sir Henry is determined to solve the mystery once and for all.

### (CURTAIN OPENS)

**Sir Henry**  Well, here we are, gentlemen, ready and waiting for the Ghost of Muddledump Manor to turn up. I'm sorry all the lights have gone out. I wonder who turned them off. Maybe it was the ghost.

**Billings**  It could have been the Electric Light Company. Have you paid your bill?

**Sir Henry**  Of course I have, you idiot. Now be quiet please. The bewitching hour of midnight approaches. Soon it will strike twelve (*All wait breathlessly. Chiming clock strikes twelve.*) Ah, midnight! Well, he shouldn't be long now.

**Muggins**  That's a nice clock you've got there, Sir Henry.

**Sir Henry**  This is no time to be referring to my face.

**Muggins**  No, I mean your chiming clock. I like cuckoo clocks myself, though. I'm having a bit of trouble with mine.

**Sir Henry**  Oh really!

**Muggins**  Yes, it's the cuckoo. He comes out and oos before he cooks.

**Sir Henry**  Silence you idiot. This is no time for jokes. Did you put the clock right, Reginald?

**Reginald**   Oh rather, father!

**Sir Henry**   And you've got the tape-recorder working?

**Reginald**   Oh rather, father!

**Sir Henry**   Did you put the new tape on?

**Reginald**   Oh rather, father!

**Sir Henry**   Splendid! Then all we have to do is wait. SHH. (*Pause 10 seconds. Creaking noises heard.*) Billings, why are you looking like that?

**Billings**   Like what?

**Sir Henry**   Like death warmed up.

**Billings**   Well, I've got a peculiar feeling coming over me. I feel uneasy. A voice within me is speaking. A queer voice deep down inside me here. What could it be?

**Muggins**   It sounds like chronic indigestion to me. I told you not to eat crayfish and pickled onions for supper.

**Sir Henry**   You're not afraid are you Billings?

**Billings**   Oh no. I always go green this time of night.

**Sir Henry**   Remember Billings, nil desperandum! We must all be brave gentlemen. Billings, you'd like to be a hero wouldn't you?

**Billings**   Yes, Sir Henry.

**Sir Henry**   You'd like people to honour your name?

**Billings**   Yes, Sir Henry.

**Sir Henry**   You'd like to go down in history, wouldn't you?

**Billings**   Yes, Sir Henry.

**Sir Henry**   Then you *will* be brave?

**Billings**   No, Sir Henry.

**Sir Henry**   But Billings, you'd like to be the idol of the people, wouldn't you? You'd like to be talked about, read about, raved about?

**Billings**   Yes, but I'd like to be *round* about while they are doing it.

(*Pause.*)

**Sir Henry**   No more jokes please, Billings. *You'll* be brave won't you Reginald?

**Reginald**   Oh rather, father.

**Sir Henry**   You always have been brave, haven't you Reginald?

**Reginald**   Oh rather, father.

**Sir Henry**   And if the ghost should be a beautiful lady, will you seize her by the arm?

**Reginald**   OH RATHER, FATHER!

(*Loud knocking noise is heard.*)

**Sir Henry**   What's that? It sounds like two things being knocked together.

**Billings**   It is. It's my knees. (*Silence of 5 seconds.*)

**Muggins**   (*shining his torch straight at **Sir Henry***) Hold still, Sir Henry. I think I can see it. It's gruesome. It's a horrible colour. And it's twined itself tightly round your neck.

**Sir Henry**   Muggins, you idiot. That's only the necktie my wife gave me last Christmas. (*Shines his torch right round the room.*) What you fellows need is some action. Let's go in different directions. And if anyone sees the ghost or anything horrible, just yell!

(*Cast all rise and start to prowl around room, flashing torches. **Muggins** and **Billings** bump into each other, back to back. They both yell and grab each other. They wrestle furiously.*)

**Muggins**   Let go, you fool. It's only me, you idiot Billings!

**Sir Henry**   Be quiet you two. SSSH.

(*They creep around for 10 seconds, then **Reginald** lets out a scream.*)

**Reginald**   Oh, it's creeping upon me! It's creeping upon me!

**Sir Henry**   What, the ghost Reginald?

**Reginald**  No father! My new woollen singlet!

(*They all prowl around for 10 seconds, then **Muggins** lets out a scream.*)

**Muggins**  I've seen it, I've seen it! I can't bear to look at it. It's glaring at me with big bloodshot eyes. It has a horrible mouth, and a ghoulish, twisted face. Oh, it's terrible. It's the most frightening thing I've ever seen!

**Sir Henry**  Muggins, you fool, come away from that wall mirror.

(*They prowl some more.*)

(*Loud bumping noise is heard on stage. **Sir Henry** goes to chair.*) Hullo, somebody's hiding under the chair. Are you there Reginald?

**Reginald**  (*from under the chair*) Oh rather, father!

**Sir Henry**  Oh, I give up. You are all afraid. I'm the only brave man amongst you. Sit down, before you fall down.

(*All sit down. Loud footsteps and a deep-throated laugh heard offstage.*)

What was that? It must be the Ghost of Muddledump Manor! Who'll go to the door and challenge him? Please don't all speak at once. (*Pause.*) Well, come on. Who'll volunteer to challenge the ghost? No one! I thought so. Then I must do the deed myself. (*He rises and goes to the door.*)

**Billings and Muggins**  Oh, be careful Sir Henry. Be careful. He may be dangerous. Don't take any chances.

**Sir Henry**  You may be right. I must act with great caution. I will just open the door slowly and peep through. (***Sir Henry** opens the door slowly and peeps through. He recoils in horror.*)

**Billings**  Can you see him, Sir Henry?

**Sir Henry**  (*Turns to rest of cast.*) Yes, Yes, I can see him. (*taking another look*) Oh, it's terrible! It's far worse than I ever imagined. He's all dressed in white. In his right hand there's a white gleaming object which is shining in the moonlight and in his left hand he is holding a flame. But I am not afraid. I shall fling wide the door and challenge him. (**Sir Henry** *flings wide the door.*) Tell me, are you the Ghost of Muddledump Manor? (*Switches on lights.*)

**Milkman** (*offstage*) The Ghost of Muddledump Manor? Don't be daft, lad. (*jumping into the room holding a milk-bottle*) I'm the milkman. How many pints do you want? (*All collapse.*)

## BLACKOUT

*Special note*  The lights must come on at the finish so that the milkman is clearly seen. If this is not possible, then all cast should shine their torches on him. The pauses throughout sketch should create tension, which is of course broken by a ridiculous remark.

## Questions

1  The play is called *The Ghost of Muddledump Manor!* The playwright has made up the word 'Muddledump'. Why do you think it is a good word to have in the title?

2  What evidence can you find to show that the characters are not very brave?

3  Describe how you would play the part of Sir Henry.

4  What comments would you make about the character of Reginald?

5  'I'm sorry all the lights have gone out.' Why is this important to the action of the play?

6  Which parts of the play did you find humorous?

7  What sound-effects would be necessary during the play?

8  Did you like the ending of the play. Why or why not?

# SNOW BRIGHT AND THE SEVEN WHARFIES.

Maureen Stewart

## Cast

**Narrator**
**Snow Bright**
**Stepmudder**
**Good Fairy**
**Huntsman**
**Elvis Geetar**
**Talking Mirror**
**Seven Wharfies**
  **Winken**
  **Blinken**
  **Stinken**
  **Nod**
  **Droopy**
  **Overtime**
  **Sleepy**
**Prince Charmpits**

**Narrator**  We wish to present our version of *Snow White and the Seven Dwarfs*. You will notice that some of the names have been changed to protect the guilty. Our first scene is at Snow Bright's pad. She is unlucky enough to live with Stepmudder, who is lucky enough to live with a young singer.

### SCENE 1

*Stepmudder* and *Elvis Geetar* are having their cornflakes. There is a large mirror on the wall.

**Stepmudder**  How come you don't talk to me any more, Elvis? You just read your paper in the mornings these days.

**Elvis**  I talk to you at night sometimes.

**Stepmudder**  If you call 'Where's my guitar?' talking, you're crazy. I think you're getting tired of me.

**Elvis**  (*grimacing behind his newspaper*) Never! After all, you're going to help me become famous. You've got all the right connections.

**Stepmudder**  But a woman needs to be told she's beautiful. Don't you know that?

**Elvis**  You're beautiful. (*He shovels his cronflakes into his mouth, and doesn't look up from his paper.*)

**Stepmudder**  Sound as though you *mean* it! Or I'll . . .

**Elvis**  Muddy, you're just *soooo* beautiful. Now I'm off. I've got an audition at the Forest Glade at ten.

(*Snow Bright* enters with the coffee.)

**Stepmudder**  And about time too, Snow Bright. I don't know, ever since your father kicked the bucket you've been a drag. Not even quick with the coffee any more.

**Elvis**  Leave the kid alone. Hi, gorgeous, how's life?

**Snow Bright**  Lousy. At least Dad gave me pocket money. All Stepmud gives me is jobs. Are you going out, Elvis?

**Elvis**  (*shovelling in the last of his cornflakes and gulping his coffee*) Yes, bright eyes. See ya around five. 'Bye, Mud. (*He rushes out.*)

**Stepmudder**  (*angry*) You ungrateful sod! That's the trouble. You take these young people in, and they never really show their gratitude. Look at you, Snow Bright. I could've kicked you out a year ago.

**Snow Bright**  People would talk.

**Stepmudder**  Well, buzz off and wash up. And make the beds. Get!

(***Snow Bright** gets. **Stepmudder** gets up and walks over to mirror.*)

Mirror mirror on the wall,
Who's the fairest one of all?

**Mirror**  Oh, not again!

**Stepmudder**  Again. I never get tired of hearing it.

**Mirror**  I'm exhausted. This goes on day and night. I'll fix her. (*loudly*) Snow Bright is the fairest one of all, Mud Face!

**Stepmudder**  No! No! (*She picks up a plate and goes to smash the **Mirror**, but she misses.*)

**Mirror**   Hey, don't do that, Mud. Then you'll never be able to find out things any more! Don't be so stupid.

**Stepmudder**   Yes, you're right. (*Thinks.*) I'll get rid of Snow Bright. Huntsman!

(**Huntsman** *runs on stage.*)

**Huntsman**   (*saluting with his gun*) At your service, Mudam.

**Stepmudder**   Take Snow Bright out into the forest and shoot her.

**Huntsman**   Done. (*yelling*) Snowy! (**Snow Bright** *runs on stage.*) Come on, kid, we're going on a picnic.

**Snow Bright**   Great! Just fix my hair, won't be a sec.

(**Huntsman** *leaves.*)

**Stepmudder**   You'll get that question again tonight, mirror.

(*The* **Mirror** *sighs.* **Stepmudder** *leaves the room.* **Narrator** *sneaks on.*)

**Narrator**   Well, kiddies, what Stepmudder doesn't know is that Snow Bright and the Huntsman are great friends, and the last thing he'd do to his favourite snakes-and-ladders partner is shoot her. He does take her on a picnic, and they discuss the whole problem. He says he has seven friends, all wharfies, who are desperate for a housekeeper, and he'll hide her there for a while. So our next scene is the wharfies' house in the forest.

## SCENE 2

*The **Seven Wharfies** are sitting on the floor with the **Huntsman** and **Snow Bright**. They are all playing marbles.*

**Winken**  Hey, Hunty, this seems like a great idea. We save this doll from death, and get ourselves a housekeeper!

**Blinken**  Can you cook sausages?

**Stinken**  Can you make cheesecakes?

**Nod**  Can you play pontoon?

**Droopy**  What time do you get up?

**Overtime**  (*to **Sleepy***) Hey, we have to go to work now.

**Sleepy**  (*asleep*) zzzzz ... (*Snores.*)

**Overtime**  Come on, Sleepy, off to work. See you at five, Snow Bright.

**Stinken**  Don't open the door to any strange men!

**Snow Bright**  No. Oh, you're so kind. Thanks so much. See you later! Sausages and chips for dinner!

**Nod**  Great. Come on, fellas, we're late. (*The **Wharfies** walk off, singing.*)

> Hi ho, hi ho, it's off to work we go,
> Work we don't like
> Might start a strike,
> Hi ho, hi ho.

(***Snow Bright** starts to tidy up the marbles, and looks happy.*)

## SCENE 3

**Narrator**  (*creeping onto the stage*) Hi there, everyone. We're back at the Stepmudder's pad now. Hey, Overtime! Come back and change the scenery!

(**Overtime** *runs on and puts the mirror on the wall.*)

Great. Now, the Huntsman came back and told Stepmud he'd shot Snow Bright. She believed him, the old crone. She decides to make herself look really beautiful (for her, that's hard) before Elvis comes home, and then to ask the mirror the same old question.

(**Narrator** *runs off, and* **Stepmudder** *walks on, straightening her eyebrows with her fingers.*)

**Stepmudder**  Wow, what a sight I'll look now. Even found her cosmetics.

(**Elvis** *enters.*)

Hi, big boy. (*She puts her hand on the hip, and walks over to him, swaying.*)

**Elvis**  Gawd, did you rob a perfume factory or something? What a smell! Yuk. (*He puts his guitar down.*) I'm tired. Got any beer? Where's Snow Bright?

**Stepmudder**  Funny you should ask that, Elvis baby. I think she's left home.

**Elvis**  Snowy? Never! Where would she go?

**Stepmudder**  Well, she's not here ...

**Elvis**  Didn't you check her room to see what she took? Are her things there?

*(He rushes out, and **Stepmudder** stares angrily after him. Then she walks over to the **Mirror**. She doesn't hear him return, and he overhears part of the conversation.)*

**Stepmudder**  Mirror mirror on the wall,
Who's the fairest one of all?

**Mirror**  I knew it. Here we go again. *Snow Bright*!

**Stepmudder**  *(screaming) What!* But she's dead!

**Mirror**  Not as dead as you, you old bat. She's living in the forest, with the seven wharfies. So there!

**Elvis**  What do you mean, dead, you old hag? You tried to have her killed, didn't you? I'm going to collect her tomorrow and bring her back. Where's my guitar?

**Stepmudder**  If you ask me where your guitar is again I'll have *you* killed!

**Elvis**  Big deal. I'm off now. Guess what, Mudface. I'm playing tonight at the rock concert. Fame at last. *(He walks off, singing.)*

**Stepmudder**  Now, let me think. There's got to be some way out of this.

*(She sits at the table, with her head in her hands. **Narrator** sneaks on.)*

**Narrator**  As usual, Stepmudder comes up with something. She decides to dress up and go to the wharfies' house the next day, and give Snow Bright a poison chocolate. Snow Bright never could resist chocolates. Then she gets a better idea . . . she'll give her a poison lipstick! That way she won't be found out, she decides.

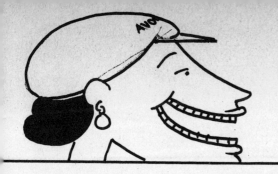

## SCENE 4

*In the **Wharfies'** house, in the forest. It is the next morning. The **Wharfies** are all asleep, and **Snow Bright** is making coffee.*

**Snow Bright**   Come on, you guys, you'll be late for work! Up you get!

**Winken**   Oh, thanks, Snowy.

**Overtime**   (*yawning*) What time is it?

**Blinken**   That's all you ever want to know, Overtime. Where's Sleepy?

**Sleepy**   Awake, you prawn.

**Nod**   Hey, it's eight-thirty! And that union meeting is at nine. Come on, fellas, let's rush. See ya, Snowy! (*They all walk out singing.*)

> Hi ho, hi ho, it's off to work we go,
> Work we don't like
> Might start a strike,
> Hi ho, hi ho.

(***Snow Bright*** *tidies up. There is soon a knock on the door.*)

**Snow Bright**   Are you a strange man?

**Stepmudder's Voice**   No. Avon calling!

**Snow Bright**   Pity. (*She shrugs, and opens the door.*)

**Stepmudder**   (*disguised as an Avon lady*) Hello there. You aren't one of my regular customers, are you?

**Snow Bright**   You're wasting your time. I have no money.

**Stepmudder**   Well, it's your lucky day! Today I'm giving away free samples ... of strawberry-tasting lipstick!

**Snow Bright**   Wow! Let me see.

**Stepmudder**   (*producing a tube of lipstick*) Here we are. It tastes as good as it looks.

**Snow Bright**   (*taking it and putting some on*) Mmmmmmm! (*She licks her lips, and faints.*)

**Stepmudder**   And about time too, you little creep.

(*She creeps out, leaving* **Snow Bright** *on the floor. But soon the* **Wharfies** *can be heard, singing. They come in.*)

**Droopy**   Hey, what have we here?

**Nod**   Snow Bright.

**Winken**   Funny, funny. What's wrong with her?

**Stinken**   Hey, come on, love! Wake up. (*Shakes* **Snow Bright**.) She won't.

**Overtime**   (*puzzled*) What's this? A tube of strawberry lipstick. Hey, I know what happened! I saw this show on telly and someone wanted to bump someone off and used a poison tube of this stuff! You can get them through mail orders in the paper. That rotten Stepmudder must have done this. Just as well there was a strike and we came home early.

**Blinken**   Yeah, I saw that show . . . wait a minute. Wasn't there an antidote?

**Overtime**   Yeah. What was it now?

**Sleepy**   Something about a prince.

**Winken**   That was it! What we have to do, fellas, is get her in a glass coffin and put her in the forest and a prince comes and kisses her and everyone lives happily ever after.

**Nod**   Quick, let's do it.

(*They carry her offstage, singing.*)

Hi ho, hi ho, it's off with her we go,
It's work we like
So we won't strike,
Hi ho, hi ho.

### SCENE 5

**Narrator**   Well, its almost over for everyone now. Stepmudder is back at her pad, talking to her mirror again. The wharfies are setting Snow Bright up for a happy ending, and Elvis Geetar has his best friend, Prince Charmpits, from a rock group, to help him find Snow Bright. Here they come. All of them. I'm off. (*He runs off. The* **Wharfies** *come on again, and put* **Snow Bright** *down. They weep noisily.*)

**Nod**   This is right, isn't it?

**Sleepy**   Yeah, it's the right ending. But in the telly play there were animals and dwarfs and things crying.

**Winken**   Animals don't cry.

**Sleepy**   These did.

**Overtime**   Shut up and get on with the crying bit. (*They cry even more noisily.* **Elvis** *and* **Prince** *come onto the stage.*)

**Elvis**   Thought I heard something like wharfies crying.

**Prince**   Yeah. It's a sound you never mistake. Hi, fellas!

**Wharfies**   Hey, aren't you Prince Charmpits? The guy who plays drums for the Purple Hearts?

**Prince**  (*proudly*) That's me!

**Blinken**  Well, kiss Snow Bright for us!

**Prince**  My pleasure. But get her lipstick off first, so I can enjoy it. (***Nod*** *rubs off her lipstick.* ***Prince*** *kisses* ***Snow Bright***.)

**Snow Bright**  (*waking up*) Oh, it's Prince Charmpits, my favourite drummer. Oh!

**Elvis**  (*watching them embrace*) He always gets the girl.

**Wharfies**  Thanks, fellas . . . Now we have to rush to a union meeting. See you! (*They walk off, singing.*)

**Elvis**  Come on, Prince. Let's all move into your place. Stepmudder's is really bad news.

## SCENE 6

**Narrator**  Actually, there is no Scene 6. But we'd just like to tell you that everything ended happily for everyone. Prince and Elvis are doing very well with their music, and Snow Bright is learning singing. We were going to kill off Stepmudder, but we hate violence, so we decided to let her pace her pad until she drops from exhaustion. What we *did* do was bribe the Mirror, so it always says she *is* the fairest of them all. That doesn't cause any trouble.

## CURTAIN

## Questions

1 As the play opens, what complaint is Stepmudder making about Elvis?

2 Why is Snow Bright unhappy about living with Stepmudder?

3 What is strange and special about the mirror on the wall?

4 Give examples to show that Mirror has a mind of its own.

5 Why does Stepmudder agree not to smash the mirror?

6 Why does Stepmudder decide to get rid of Snow Bright?

7 How does she plan to do this?

8 The Narrator explains why the Huntsman saves Snow Bright. What is the reason the Narrator puts forward?

9 With whom does Snow Bright stay in the forest?

10 When the Seven Wharfies go off to work they leave Snow Bright with a warning. What is it?

11 How does Elvis find out that Stepmudder has tried to kill Snow Bright?

12 What is Elvis's nickname for Stepmudder?

13 The Wharfies decide that there is an antidote to the poison. What is it?

14 How does everything end happily for everyone?

15 Can you say what the main points of difference are between this play and the original tale?

16 Why is this play humorous, whereas the original story of Snow White and the Seven Dwarfs is not?

# Numbers at the Gate

### Bill Condon and Dianne Bates

## Cast

**Radio Announcer**
**Molly Slack**
**Numbers Galore**
**Rita St Peter**
**Hugh McClue**
**Mirabelle Swellbottom**
**Firmen Gryp**
**St Peter**
**Angela Generous**
**Dougal McFrugal**
**Chastity del Brido**
**Hope Chest**
**Ethelready Wise**
**Dave Brave**
**Justice Rules**

### SCENE 1

*At the gates of Heaven. The gates, placed in the middle of the stage, are securely locked with a padlock. Behind the gates is a desk with chair. The stage is empty. Soft music is playing but it is interrupted suddenly by the sounds of news pips.*

**Radio Announcer**  We interrupt this programme to bring you the following newsflash: Five people were gunned down this afternoon during an armed hold-up at the Downtown City Bank. The notorious gangsters Numbers Galore and Molly Slack were among those killed. More details in the 6 p.m. news.

(*The music resumes, then fades as* **Molly** *enters stealthily, looking around her.*)

**Molly**  It's all clear, Numbers!

(**Numbers** *enters, carrying a machine-gun; he begins to check the place out. Then he sits down in front of the gates and broods.*)

Gee, Numbers, this is a really nice place — we could be happy here . . . (*She looks at the gate.*) Wow, that's real gold! I bet you'd get a lot of wedding rings out of that. . . . Numbers, are you listening? What's the matter with ya?

**Numbers**  What's the matter with me? . . . That's the first time I've ever been killed, and if I have my way, it's gunna be the last. . . . I just don't like it.

**Molly**  Aw come on, Numbers, when your number's up, it's up!

**Numbers**  That dirty flatfoot McClue. He fired when I wasn't ready . . .

**Molly**  Oh well, we'll just have to make the most of it, sweetheart.

**Numbers**  Did you say something about gold?

**Molly**  Yeah, this gate's full of gold.

**Numbers**  That's not gold, dummy, it's pearls.

**Molly**  Who's Pearl? One of your girlfriends, is she?

**Numbers**  No, you idiot, it's the Pearly Gates!

**Molly**   Then we're here ... we made it, Numbers! All my life I dreamed of this.... Oh, so this is Hell!

**Numbers**   Molly, come here...

**Molly**   What, Numbers?

**Numbers**   (*whispering*) I got something to tell you, Moll.

**Molly**   (*whispering*) What?

**Numbers**   (*speaking slowly*) This is Heaven!

(***Molly*** *hesitates a moment.*)

**Molly**   Oh, Numbers, that's the most romantic thing you've ever said to me.... Me being here with you *is* Heaven ... oooh....

**Numbers**   I told you to turn left back there. You said you had a great sense of direction.

**Molly**   I do, I do. (*Pause.*) But I lost it.

**Numbers**   Hey, wait a minute, I just thought of something ...

**Molly**   What?

**Numbers**   Them gates. If they're pearls, just imagine what's inside them. Hey! We could be rich, Moll!

**Molly**   We could buy that little house on the hill ... and have a family ... three kids ... five kids!

**Numbers**   A canary ... a golden canary!

**Molly**   Let's ring the doorbell, Numbers.

**Numbers**   Do you think they're just gunna hand over the goodies, Moll? This is a heist, the big job I been waiting for all my life. All them rich people that get to Heaven just waiting to be robbed. Give me my tools, Moll.

(***Molly*** *hands him a hairpin. He has trouble picking the lock.*)

I don't know what's wrong. It's never failed before. (*He suddenly realizes.*) This is a left-handed hairpin, Moll.

**Molly**   Oh. I left all my right-handers at the bank, Numbers.

**Numbers**  You don't know your left from your right ...

**Molly**  I do too. That's my left hand ... that's where the wedding ring goes, Numbers ...

**Numbers**  There's nothing for it — we gotta get help.

**Molly**  How?

**Numbers**  Hell.

**Molly**  Numbers, watch your language!

**Numbers**  We gotta go to Hell. That's where all me mates are. They'll have tools. Come on, Moll.

**Molly**  But I thought this *was* Hell ...

## SCENE 2

*The gates of Heaven have been slid open. There is a queue of three waiting to get in. Mrs* **Rita St Peter** *is seated at the desk, writing in a big book.*

**Radio Announcer**    (*voice-over*) A further update on the armed robbery this morning at the Downtown City Bank. Gunned down (*fade-out*) were ...

**Rita**    Name please.

**Hugh**    Hugh McClue.

**Rita**    I'm Rita St Peter, St Peter's mother. Little Pete's mum.

**Hugh**    How do you do ... I'm Detective Sergeant Hugh McClue. (*He shows his badge and gestures towards the others.*) We came together.

**Mirabelle**    And I'm Mirabelle Swellbottom. *Miss* Mirabelle Swellbottom. (*She is carrying an umbrella and dumbbells.*)

**Firmen**    Firmen Gryp, Banker. (*He shakes hands with* **Rita**.)

**Rita**    Let's see now ... we've got ... Glue, Bellbottom and Swell.

**Hugh**    No, I'm McClue ...

**Mirabelle**    Swellbottom, Miss ...

**Firmen**    Gryp, Firmen ...

**Rita**    That's what I said ...

> (*There is confusion; each person continues to protest.*)

> Oh dear, oh dear. Just a minute, I'll get my son Peter St Peter ... he's second in charge, he'll know what to do. (*She picks up a harp and plucks it. It rings like a telephone.*)

**Voice-over**    Number please.

**Rita**    123 4567, connect me please with St Peter in Heaven.

**Mirabelle**    I tell you — if I ever catch that young man who shot me down, why, I'll hit him with my umbrella, just like I was doing in the bank.

**Firmen**  He didn't even have an account . . . let alone the fact that he wasn't a regular customer!

**Rita**  Peter, I'm in an awful dither down here. . . . It's Swell, Bell and Gluebottom, and they're not what they seem. Do you think He could spare you for a few minutes?

**St Peter**  (*voice-over*) Coming, Mother!

(**McClue** *has been looking about. He is inspecting the gates of Heaven.*)

**Hugh**  Hullo, hullo, hullo . . . What have we here?

**Firmen**  Something of interest, McClue?

**Hugh**  Ye gods and little fishes! It can't be . . .

**Mirabelle**  Who's a little vicious? That young man in the bank, surely!

**Hugh**  There's hairpin prints on this lock. I'd know that trademark anywhere . . . it's that gangster Galore. He's been here!

**Firmen**   That man will have to account for his actions.

**Mirabelle**   That vicious gangster, trying to break into Heaven! . . .
When I catch up with him, there'll be hell to pay!

(*St Peter enters. He is carrying a booklet.*)

**St Peter**   Hell hath no fury . . . Hullo, Mother.

**Rita**   Hullo, dear. Yes, I remember Fury — he was such a dear
horse . . . and Black Beauty and Phar Lap and Lassie . . .

**Hugh**   (*to St Peter*) I have reason to believe there's been an attempted
gate-napping . . .

**St Peter**   Napping? Napping? I never sleep on the job.

**Rita**   Someone's tried to steal the gates, Peter.

**Firmen**   Are you in charge here? You've got to get me back, sir. I
didn't balance the books before I left.

**Mirabelle**   And I have a weightlifting class at 2 p.m.

(*The action freezes as **Molly** and **Numbers** enter.*)

**Numbers**   They didn't remember me! We used to be as thick as
thieves!

**Molly**   Aw Numbers, you're still the thickest thief I know.

**Numbers**   Thanks a lot, Moll.

**Molly**   Any time, Big Boy.

**Numbers**   We gotta knock off these Pearly Gates somehow . . .

**Molly**   Why don't you go straight, Numbers; turn over a new leaf and
be a Good Samaritan?

**Numbers**   Are you kiddin'? I could never survive a samarathon.

(*The others on stage unfreeze and begin to talk. There is a general
babble.*)

**Molly**   Numbers, I hear voices.

**Numbers**   Me too.

**Firmen**   I have to get back, St Peter — I have ten thousand dollars in my pocket which I forgot to deposit.

**Molly and Numbers**   Ten thousand!!!

**Firmen**   I *think* it was ten thousand ... plus a few dollars I scooped up during the hold-up — they were making the place look untidy. Look, I'll just sit down and count them. It'll give me something to do. (*He begins counting and continues doing this during the following scene.*) One thousand ...

**Hugh**   I smell a rat!

**Numbers**   Them's fightin' words. Get him, Moll!

(**Molly** *advances towards* **Hugh McClue** *and hits him. At the same time* **Mirabelle Swellbottom** *recognizes* **Numbers**.)

**Mirabelle**   You're the young man who held up the bank ... (*She advances threateningly.*)

**Numbers**   Oh no, that crazy old dame with the umbrella.

(*He squares off. She lifts her dumbbell and umbrella at him.* **Molly** *continues to jab at* **McClue** *and gets him in a headlock.*)

**Hugh**   You're under arrest, Galore.

**Firmen**   Twenty-six thousand four hundred and twenty-five dollars ...

**Rita**   STOP! (*She plucks her harp, which produces a gong sound.*) It seems we have a little problem here ...

**Mirabelle**   They've got no right to be in Heaven.

**Rita**   It looks like it's a union matter ... Peter!

(**St Peter** *is reading the form-guide booklet,* The Angel Trots.)

**Hugh**   What's the chance of these low-down violent blackguards staying here?

**Numbers**   Violent? Who's he calling 'violent'? Hit him, Moll.

(**Molly**, *however, still has* **Hugh McClue** *in a headlock. She twists his nose.* **Mirabelle** *pins* **Numbers** *by the neck with her dumbbell.*)

**St Peter**   (*finally looking up from his form-guide*) I can get you 5 to 1. Best odds you'll get anywhere in Heaven.

**Rita**   Call the union, Peter.

**St Peter**   Ah, H.A.R.P.S., Mother! (*He snaps his fingers.*)

**Molly**   Don't be so unkind to your mother.

**Rita**   The Heavenly Association for the Rehabilitation of Prolific Sinners. H.A.R.P.S.

**Firmen**   Thirty-eight thousand five hundred and ninety-three dollars ...

(*Seven* **Angels** *appear. They curtsy to* **St Peter**.)

**Rita**  Introducing, the Seven HARPS!

**Angela**  Angela Generous.

**Dougal**  Dougal McFrugal.

**Chastity**  Chastity del Brido.

**Hope**  Hope Chest.

**Ethelready**  Ethelready Wise.

**Dave**  Dave Brave.

**Justice**  Justice Rules.

> (*They line up in choir fashion, clasping their hands as if in prayer. They sing.*)

**HARPS**   (*to the tune of 'Jingle Bells'*)

> HARPS we are,
> HARPS we are,
> HARPS we are in Heaven;
> When union strife is in your life
> Call on the Heavenly Seven . . .

(*There is a general babble among the others on stage. But **St Peter** is preoccupied — he is still reading the form-guide. And **Firmen Gryp** is still counting money.*)

**Justice**   (*playing harp to produce the sound of a gong being struck*) Order! Order!

**Molly**   Two meat pies. With sauce, please!

**Numbers**   Here comes the judge!

**Firmen**   Fifty-seven thousand six hundred and forty-two dollars . . .

**Justice**   Mr Justice Rules presiding. (*He looks around smiling.*) Just call me J.R. Now, what seems to be the problem, St Peter?

(***St Peter*** *is still reading his form-guide.*)

**Mirabelle**   They've got no right to be in Heaven, your majesty.

**Hugh**   This man, this Numbers Galore, has got the longest criminal record of any man on earth.

**Molly**   Don't that make you feel proud, Numbers?

**Numbers**   Yes, and to think I did all this . . . and may I say, not in a shy way . . . (*He begins to sing and the **HARPS** join in.*) Oh no, not I, I did it my way.

**Rita**   Do you do requests, Mr Galore?

**Justice**   Now, it seems to me from the evidence presented by . . . (*He looks askance at **Mirabelle** and **Hugh**.*)

**Hugh**   Hugh McClue — Detective Sergeant.

**Mirabelle**   Mirabelle Swellbottom — Miss.

**Justice**   Yes, it seems to me that (*pointing to **Numbers***) this man and his wife. . .

**Molly**   Oh Numbers, he's just pronounced us man and wife!!!

**Numbers**   Hell!

> (*The seven **HARPS** are shocked. They cover their eyes and ears, and they mouth the word to each other.*)

**Justice**   ... and his friend ... are being accused of crimes committed while on earth ...

**Hugh**   Ghastly crimes ...

**Mirabelle**   Horrible crimes ...

**Numbers**   When you've got it, why not flaunt it?

**Justice**   Does anyone here wish to speak in defence of the accused?

**Molly**   I do.

**Justice**   Inadmissible.

**Firmen**   Eighty-nine thousand one hundred and twenty-six dollars ...

**Justice**   You sir, you have something to say?

**Molly**   Him! Ask him how he got the money ...

**Justice**
**Mirabelle** } Well?
**Hugh**

**Firmen**   Um ... ah ... I had this paper run ...?

**Molly**   He's just as much a robber as we are ...

**Hugh**   She's right, you know. You should be arrested, Gryp.

**Numbers**   Why don't you tell them about the good old days, McClue? When we were partners ...

**Molly**   I remember that. They were in the jewellery business. The newspapers called them —

(**St Peter** *looks up from his form-guide.*)

**St Peter**   ... the Smash and Grab Brothers.

(*They all look at* **St Peter**.)

We get the papers up here — we don't miss anything. We've been watching you, sir. (*He looks accusingly at* **McClue**.)

**Hugh**  But I reformed, didn't I? Not like him.... Or her....

**Rita**  But that's the purpose of the Heavenly Association for the Rehabilitation of Prolific Sinners.

**Angela**  We'll put Numbers Galore and Molly Slack ...

**Dougal**  On the right path ...

**Chastity**  And on the right track.

**Hope**  We'll see that they're free ...

**Ethelready**  From Sin forever ...

**Dave**  Sinners once — but again ...?

**HARPS**  (*in chorus*) Never!!

**Justice**  Mr Galore, and ... your sister, is it?

**Molly**  Fiancée!

**Justice**  HARPS has decided that you are at liberty to enter the Kingdom of Heaven, providing there are no objections. (*Looks around.*)

**Numbers**  I'm free, I beat the wrap!

**Mirabelle**  I object!

**Molly**  Oh come on, love, give us a chance. All we wanted was to get enough money to settle down and raise a family, and ...

**Mirabelle**  Very well, my dear. I'll forgive you. Young man, I'll withdraw my objection provided you do the right thing by your fiancée.

**Justice**  A marriage made in Heaven.

**Molly**  Oh, Numbers!

**Numbers**  Oh, Hell!

**Voice-over**  One marriage, coming up.

(*Organ music: 'Here Comes the Bride'. All begin to exit as music continues.*)

**Firmen**  And tell me, St Peter, do you have banks in Heaven?

**Mirabelle**  Actually, I think I'm getting too old for weightlifting. Do you have hang-gliding up here, Mrs St Peter?

**Rita**  No, but we have cloud-hopping.

**Mirabelle**  Oh lovely, I haven't tried that yet.

(**Molly** *and* **Numbers** *are the last to leave*.)

**Molly**  At last! You're gunna go straight, Numbers.

**Numbers**  (*muttering to himself*) Marriage ... marriage ...

(*Just after they exit, the music is suddenly interrupted by a series of beeps.*)

**Radio Announcer**  (*voice-over*) Good afternoon. This is Radio 2 G.O.D., your celestial station, bringing you the midday news. The headlines: A daring hold-up of a second-hand halo shop in High Street, Heaven, dominates today's stories ...

(*Fade-out.*)

*CURTAIN*

## Questions

1 What scenery would be necessary for the staging of *Numbers at the Gate*?

2 Why do you think the play is called *Numbers at the Gate*?

3 What is the attitude of Numbers towards Hugh McClue?

4 Imagine you have been selected to play the part of Numbers in a school production of the play. How would you dress? What aspects of his character would you try to bring out for the audience?

5 What comments would you make about the character of Firmen Gryp?

6 What are some things you might consider unusual about the St Peter depicted in *Numbers at the Gate*?

7 '... I'll hit him with my umbrella, just like I was doing in the bank.' What do these words reveal about Mirabelle's character?

8 Which part of the play did you enjoy most? Why?

# THE FORTRESS

(A Drama)

### Allan Mackay

---

**Cast**

**Madame Garrard**
**Margaret,** *her granddaughter*
**Henri,** *her servant*
**Jean Renaud**
**Marcel**
**Sergeant Baras**

---

## Introduction

*The Fortress* is a drama probably best suited for more advanced classes in the junior school. It presents, in a relatively minor incident, an understatement of the thesis that war causes the destruction of more than life and property: it undermines and destroys values that are essential to man's personal dignity and contentment. Most important of these values is love, not only for other people, but for a way of life built up painstakingly over a number of years, and for the structures that go to make up that way of life.

The focus of the dramatic action is Madame Garrard. She should occupy the centre of the stage, never shifting from that spot, while the subsidiary characters move around her, subject to her stronger will and more dominant personality. The sound-effects at the end are essential to the effect of the whole. Finally, it is hoped that the play will be a starting-point for discussion on the wider issues of man's continual madness on the field of battle.

## SCENE

*France, 1940. The drawing-room of a large villa, set high on a hill overlooking a village thirty kilometres north of Paris. It is late morning.* **Madame Garrard**, *elderly but alert and straight-backed, sits in a large chair facing the audience, an opened book on her lap. For a moment she sits in silence staring through the window, which faces the front of the house. The heavy curtains are drawn well back. Some noise outside has attracted her attention. Behind her is an open door into the hallway.*

*Feet are heard on the stairs in the hallway and* **Margaret**, *Madame Garrard's twenty-four-year-old granddaughter, rushes into the room.*

**Margaret**   Grandmother, there are soldiers — out in the garden! I saw them from the top window! And they have a truck —

**Madame G.**   Indeed. Come away from the window, now. It hardly seems proper to stare, even if they are soldiers.

**Margaret**   But grandmother —

**Madame G.**   (*firmly*) Come away!

(**Margaret** *slowly walks over to the old woman.*)

France may be at war but that's no excuse for *us* to forget our manners. Now, if you will please call Henri.

(**Margaret** *goes to the door to the hall.*)

**Margaret**   (*loudly*) Henri!

**Madame G.**   Quietly, Margaret, quietly! Henri is not in England, nor is he hard of hearing.

(**Margaret** *comes back into the room as* **Henri**, *Madame Garrard's old servant, appears at the door.*)

**Henri**   Yes, Madame?

**Madame G.**   Henri, it appears we are soon to have guests.

**Henri**   Guests, Madame?

**Madame G.**   Members of our armed forces, I believe.

(*There is a loud banging at the outer door.*)

Ah, there they are now. You may admit them.

(**Henri** *turns to go.*)

And Henri? They may be uninvited but please treat them with courtesy.

**Henri**   Of course, Madame. (**Henri** *disappears into the hallway.*)

**Margaret**   Grandmother, what do they want?

**Madame G.**   Perhaps you'd better ask them that yourself. Come, stand by me. You won't be harmed, I promise you.

(**Henri** *ushers in* **Jean** *and* **Marcel**, *two privates in uniform. They are both very young and ill at ease in the job they have to do.*)

**Henri**   The . . . soldiers, Madame.

**Madame G.** Thank you, Henri. You may remain. Good morning, gentlemen. Please come in. I'm sorry I must call you gentlemen, but I have no idea of the ranks in the French army.

(*The two soldiers nervously enter the room.* **Henri** *remains just inside the door.* **Margaret** *stands beside her grandmother.*)

I am Madame Garrard. This is my granddaughter, Margaret, and my servant, Henri. May I offer you some refreshment?

**Jean** Madame, we have orders to evacuate all civilians from this area.

**Madame G.** Evacuate, young man?

**Jean** Take you to a safer area. We're moving the entire village ... it's our orders, Madame.

**Madame G.** In heaven's name, why?

**Jean** The German army has overrun our positions twenty kilometres north of here.

**Madame G.** Ah, yes — last night I heard the guns.

**Jean** From our latest reports, a tank division is advancing in this direction.

**Madame G.** Then surely you must stop them.

**Jean**   We don't have the strength, Madame. We must all retreat.

**Madame G.**   But the Germans would not harm us. We're not very dangerous.

**Marcel**   (*impatiently*) Madame, you don't understand. The German army is striking towards Paris and we are helpless before them. Already several towns they have captured near the border have been burnt and destroyed. Civilians, like yourself, hundreds of them, have been shot for disobeying the smallest command. Others are herded into public halls and kept prisoner, many separated from their families. You must leave, for your own sakes.

**Madame G.**   They have — shot the people who are not soldiers?

**Marcel**   Yes, when they have resisted.

**Madame G.**   How can an ordinary French farmer resist the whole German army?

**Jean**   Many have, Madame. They join the Resistance.

**Madame G.**   And shoot Germans in return, no doubt.

**Marcel**   Madame, there is no time for this!

**Margaret**   Please grandmother, we must go!

**Madame G.**   So it seems. Where will you take us in your truck?

**Jean**   To Villeneuve, fifteen kilometres along the road.

**Madame G.**   And when Villeneuve is taken?

**Jean**   To Paris, I suppose.

**Madame G.**   Where we will all finally be shot — for resisting.

**Marcel**   Madame, try to realize that time is of utmost importance. In twenty minutes, even less, the tanks will be here.

**Madame G.**   Twenty minutes! Is our France to be so easily beaten?

**Jean**   Our divisions are massing at the river south of the village. Against the tanks — it seems hopeless — but if we can delay them just enough to give Paris time to prepare ...

**Marcel**  Please pack some clothing and food and come with us. I'm sorry, but it is our orders.

**Henri**  Shall I attend to it, Madame?

**Madame G.**  No, Henri. I'm sorry, young man, but I must refuse your invitation.

**Margaret**  Grandmother, no!

**Marcel**  Don't you place any value on your life — or the lives of these people?

**Madame G.**  Of course I'm speaking only for myself. Margaret will go with you.

**Margaret**  I won't! I couldn't leave you!

**Jean**  Why are you doing this?

**Madame G.**  Young man — I'm sorry, I don't know what else to call you —

**Jean**  Jean. Jean Renaud.

**Madame G.**  Mr Renaud, then — I am seventy-three years old and this house has been my home for fifty of those years. I was brought here as a bride and it was here that I bore my children and cared for my husband until he died. And — God willing — it is here that I will die. All the memories that I love are within these four walls — and to an old lady memories are all that are left to her. So you see, I cannot go with you. That is, unless you can arrange to take my house as well. And I doubt if the whole French army can manage that.

**Marcel**  We have instructions, Madame, to use force if necessary — for your own good.

**Madame G.**  Force? On me? My goodness, you are indeed fierce warriors.

**Marcel**  Jean, we're wasting time.

(*He steps forward but* **Henri**, *moving surprisingly quickly, intervenes.*)

**Henri**  I must ask you, sir, to leave this house immediately.

**Marcel**   Old man, I don't want to hurt you!

**Madame G.**   Thank you, Henri. (**Henri** *steps back*.) According to my doctor, my heart can't stand the least bit of excitement. And believe me, if the French army lays one finger on me, I'll resist them to the last breath.

**Margaret**   Please, Mr Renaud, she's speaking the truth.

**Jean**   Marcel, perhaps you'd better get the sergeant.

**Marcel**   But this is ridiculous — oh, very well, but this is on your head, Jean. (*He strides out*.)

**Madame G.**   I'm sorry that you must bear the blame for one stubborn old lady.

**Jean**   We could have used such stubbornness in the last battle.

**Madame G.**   Come now, I'm sure you all fought like heroes. How old are you, Jean?

**Jean**   Twenty.

**Madame G.**   And where are your parents?

**Jean**   I have none. They died in the French Rhineland in 1935.

**Madame G.**   That is a sad thing. No family at all?

**Jean**   One brother. He is stationed in Paris.

**Madame G.**   I had a son — Margaret's father. His name was Jean too. He and his wife were killed in 1917.

**Jean**   I'm sorry.

**Madame G.**   It was all a long time ago. But it is here in this room that I remember them best. They lived with us then and worked the vineyards on the hillside with my husband. Ah, they were warm times, those wonderful springs — but memories, memories, that's all. You're too young to have memories, Jean.

**Jean**   I remember only the battle ... and my friends dying.

**Margaret**   Were you so easily beaten, Mr Renaud?

**Jean**  We didn't have a chance. It was their guns, guns such as we had never seen. And the tanks — they cut through our positions like sharp knives —

(**Marcel** and **Sergeant Baras** enter.)

**Baras**  Renaud, you had your orders!

**Jean**  I'm sorry, sir.

**Madame G.**  Come, Sergeant, don't be too hard on Mr Renaud. I doubt if your army taught him how to capture old ladies.

**Baras**  Madame, I must insist on your leaving this house with my men — at once!

**Madame G.**  And I must refuse. If you attempt to use force, I will defend myself. Henri!

**Henri**  Yes, Madame?

**Madame G.**  Hand me my cane.

(**Henri** hands her a long wooden cane from beside her chair.)

Stand by my side. You will be my army.

**Henri**  Certainly, Madame.

**Madame G.**  And now, Sergeant — (She waves the cane in front of her.)

**Margaret**  Grandmother, don't do this!

**Madame G.**  Stand back, Margaret!

**Baras**  This is insane! You are aware that the German army —

**Madame G.**  Is just over the next hill — I know. But I'm not afraid of the German army.

**Baras**  Madame, we are at war!

**Madame G.**  Your war, Sergeant, not mine.

**Baras**  Unfortunately, the Germans make no such distinctions.

**Madame G.**  Then I will fight them with my own weapons.

**Baras**  (scornfully) You have no weapons.

**Madame G.**   If you will notice, I seem to be holding off the French army with my — weapons.

**Jean**   Please, Madame Garrard, if you stay here you will be shot.

**Madame G.**   Piffle! I'm not worth one good German bullet.

**Margaret**   Grandmother, I think we'd better go. It's for the best.

**Madame G.**   You don't understand, Margaret.

**Margaret**   But I do, I do! This house — I know what it means to you. Grandfather, and father — it's *their* house. But I'm afraid.

**Madame G.**   For yourself, child?

**Margaret**   And for you. I don't want to see you killed.

**Madame G.**   What do you think, Henri?

**Henri**   Madame, you must do what is best.

**Madame G.**   Best — yes. Perhaps you are right, Sergeant.

**Baras**   Good, good. We've wasted enough time.

(*He turns to* **Marcel**.)

You place the dynamite. Fifteen-minute fuses. With any luck we'll catch some of them in here, so hide the charges.

**Marcel**   Yes, sir. (*He goes out.*)

**Baras**   (*to* **Jean**) And you — search the house. Destroy any radios and useful foodstuffs. Get on with it!

**Jean**   Yes, sir. (*He follows* **Marcel** *out.*)

**Madame G.**   Sergeant, what are you doing?

**Baras**   Only what is necessary.

**Madame G.**   Does that include blowing up my house?

**Baras**   Yes, it does. You see, your villa is on a hill overlooking the village. From the top window you can see ten kilometres up and down the road.

**Madame G.**   I know this.

**Baras**   Then it must be obvious to you that the house would be valuable to the Germans as an observation post. We must prevent this.

**Madame G.**   But, dynamite ... everything?

**Baras**   Those are my orders.

**Madame G.**   Do your orders give you the right to use your terrible weapons on my house?

**Baras**   The war does.

**Madame G.**   But you don't know what you will destroy here.

**Baras**   Ah, but I do. I will destroy an enemy observation post.

   (*There is a long pause as they stare at each other.*)

This is your servant?

**Madame G.**   Yes.

**Baras**   (*to* **Henri**) See to Madame's belongings. Just some warm clothes will do.

**Henri**   (*hesitating*) Madame?

**Baras**   Hurry, man!

**Madame G.**   Stay where you are, Henri. Sergeant, I am not going with you. I am staying here — in my house.

**Baras**   But you said —

**Madame G.**   No, it is what you said that matters.

   (**Jean** *hurries through the door.*)

**Jean**   No radio, Sergeant, and very little food. I destroyed what there was.

**Baras**   Good. Stay here — I may need you.

**Jean**   (*surprised*) Won't she come?

**Baras**   No!

**Jean**   Madame, what about your granddaughter? Surely you can't let her stay.

**Madame G.**   Of course not.

**Margaret**   I won't go without you!

**Madame G.**   You will because I ask you.

**Margaret**   You can't make me! None of you can make me!

**Madame G.**   Margaret, you are very young and all your life is in front of you. You can't waste it on an old woman.

**Margaret**   Grandmother, please....

**Madame G.**   Henri, take Margaret with you to the truck.

**Henri**   I beg your pardon, Madame, but my place is here with you.

**Madame G.**   No Henri, I don't expect it of you. Go with them.

**Henri**   Madame, I have served this household for thirty years. So, unless you wish to dispense with my services ...

**Madame G.**   Of course not, Henri.

**Henri**   Then, with your permission, I shall withdraw and prepare lunch. I believe our young soldier friend may have overlooked a few things —

**Baras**   (*exasperated*) Lunch! At a time like this? Are you all insane?

**Madame G.**   *You* can ask us that? You with your guns and dynamite and lost battles!

(**Marcel** *rushes in.*)

**Marcel**   Sergeant — the tanks!

**Baras**   How far?

**Marcel**   About two kilometres. Footsoldiers behind.

**Baras**   They must have seen the house and our truck! How long have we got, would you say?

**Marcel**   Ten minutes, no more. They won't use the cannons.

**Baras**   And the dynamite.

**Marcel**   Set, sir. Two bundles on the top floor and two in the basement.

**Baras**   Fuses?

**Marcel**   Fifteen minutes.

**Baras**   That's cutting it a bit fine. Are they lit?

**Marcel**   No, sir.

**Baras**   Do it. We'll get the old lady out of here.

**Jean**   Wait, Sergeant, there's no need to use force. I think I can persuade Madame to leave. And I'll light the fuses.

**Baras**   Very well. I've got no time to argue. (*He goes to the door.*) The truck leaves in five minutes! (*He goes. He can be heard giving orders outside.*)

**Jean**   Marcel, take the young lady to the truck.

**Margaret**   No!

**Madame G.**   Yes, Margaret, yes! Just this once. For my sake — and your father's.

**Margaret**   But will you come?

**Madame G.**   Yes, I will come. Let me just say goodbye to my house.

(*Marcel* takes *Margaret* to the door.)

**Marcel**   We'll wait in the truck. Jean — two minutes.

**Jean**   Where are the charges?

**Marcel**   The upstairs ones are under the bed in the main room. The others are behind the stairs in the basement.

(*Marcel* and *Margaret* go out. *Jean* goes to the window, looks out.)

**Jean**   (*after a moment*) That was a lie, Madame. You don't intend to move.

**Madame G.**   Was it now? And tell me, Jean, how do you intend to persuade me?

**Jean**   (*turning to her*) I'm sure I can't, Madame.

**Madame G.**   Ah, then we are both liars.

**Jean**   Madame, I'll have to light the fuses.

**Madame G.**   Yes, the fuses. Do it quickly before I begin to beg you.

(*Jean* hurries out.)

Henri, there's still time for you.

**Henri**   I could not, Madame.

**Madame G.**   Thank you. (*She pauses.*) What will happen . . . when the dynamite explodes?

**Henri**   I think . . . it will be very quick. . . .

**Madame G.**   Are you afraid?

**Henri**   Yes.

**Madame G.**   And am I to blame?

**Henri**   Only for giving me the choice, Madame. But it was I who made it.

**Madame G.**   Do you think I should warn the Germans?

**Henri**   Madame, I would not like to think that this house is guilty of murder.

**Madame G.**   No. It would be a sorry thing and I couldn't bear it. Just as I couldn't bear to see my home turned to rubble before my eyes and boots and tanks stumble over its bricks —

(*Jean comes running in.*)

**Jean**   Fifteen minutes, Madame. There's no turning back.

**Madame G.**   Goodbye, Jean.

**Jean**   Goodbye, Madame Garrard.

**Madame G.**   Do you understand now?

**Jean**   Yes, yes, I do. Goodbye, Henri.

(*Marcel appears for a moment at the door.*)

**Marcel**   Jean, the truck's going! Hurry! (*He disappears.*)

**Madame G.**   Take care of Margaret.

**Jean**   She will be safe, I promise you. Goodbye.

(*He goes out. Henri crosses to the window and looks out. There is the sound of a truck pulling out. Slowly Henri pulls the curtains across.*)

**Madame G.**   How long do we have?

**Henri**   Only a few minutes.

**Madame G.**   So little time. Do you remember, Henri? Every morning, just after dawn, Jean would go out to the vineyards. I could see him from the top window, tall and strong above the vines, catching the grapes in his hands. It was as though he held up part of the earth for me to see. . . .

**Henri**   Yes, Madame, I remember.

(*The rumble of tanks can now be distinctly heard. Both of the old people seem not to listen.*)

**Madame G.**   Henri, do you think you might take my hand?

(**Henri** *crosses and takes her hand.*)

They could not see the vineyards from the front of the house. My son always believed that the grapes grew best on the southern slopes of the hill, so he planted them there. Let me see, now, that was in the spring of 1913, just before the Germans came —

(*But the rumble of the tanks drowns out her voice.*)

### CURTAIN

## Questions

1  What evidence can you find in the play to show that the German army is superior to the French army?

2  How does the German army treat civilians?

3  Why is there a need for Madame Garrard, Henri and Margaret to leave the villa quickly?

4  Why does Madame Garrard refuse to go to Villeneuve?

5  What kind of a person is Madame Garrard?

**6**  Why is it necessary for Jean and Marcel to blow up the villa?

**7**  What lie does Madame Garrard tell her granddaughter? Why does Madame Garrard lie?

**8**  Why do you think Henri decides to remain with Madame Garrard?

**9**  What do you think about Madame Garrard's decision to share the fate of her villa?

**10**  How would you dress if you were playing the part of (a) Marcel (b) Henri (c) Madame Garrard?

**11**  What scenery and stage props would you need in order to stage *The Fortress*?

**12**  Describe how you would play the part of one of these characters: (a) Baras (b) Madame Garrard (c) Margaret (d) Henri.

# HISS THE VILLAIN!

## or, Foiled and Counterfoiled
### (A Melodrama in One Act)

Adapted from *The Poor of New York* by
## A.R. Taylor and W. Ernest Cossons

---

### Cast

**Silas Snaker,** *a rascally banker*
**Bowler,** *his clerk*
**Captain Noble,** *an old sea captain*
**Mrs Noble,** *his wife*
**Lucy,** *their daughter*
**Percy,** *their son*
**Harold,** *their friend*

---

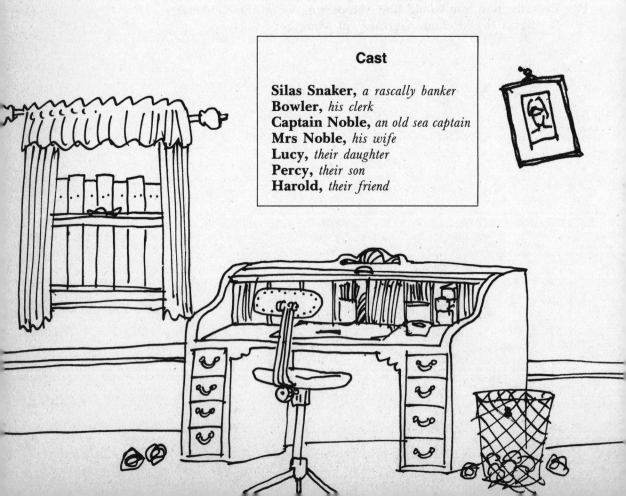

## Introduction

The villain of this play is the terrible Snaker, who is not only a thief
and a liar, but also a potential murderer. The hero is the noble Bowler,
who, although he is Snaker's accomplice at the very beginning of the
play, becomes a reformed character, determined to see justice done and
Snaker 'utterly foiled'.

## *SCENE 1*

**Snaker**'s *office. The scene can be played in front of a backcloth representing an
office, or curtains. Up centre-stage is a Victorian desk and stool. Upstage R is a
safe. By the safe is a portmanteau.*

*Before the play begins, sinister music is heard.*

*When the curtain rises the stage is empty. After a moment,* **Snaker** *enters L.
He is followed by a green spotlight as he advances to the front of the stage. When
he speaks the music fades.*

**Snaker** Fortune favours the brave! An hour ago I was bankrupt. Every stock in which I invested is down. My last effort to retrieve my fortune had plunged me into utter ruin. Tomorrow the streets of London, now so still, would have been filled with a howling multitude. The house of Snaker — the great, respected house of Snaker, the banker — would have fallen, and in falling would crush the hundreds, the thousands of simple folk who have entrusted their pitiful savings to me.

(*There are boos.*)

And with it would have gone my darling daughter, my innocent, my motherless Alice, but for one stroke of fortune. Just as I was about to bid farewell to the scene of my triumphs and my failure, and to escape, disguised as a musician, in comes a simple old sailor, Captain Noble, in his hands ten thousand pounds in gold. He hands them over to me for safe keeping before he departed on a long voyage, so that in the event of his not returning, his wife and his two children might be safe. Poor trusting fool! Poor trusting fool! Yet, why should I pity him? With his ten thousand pounds I can start afresh.

(*There are boos.*)

I can make *my* child, my Alice, safe from want. Noble's children must starve if need be. *Mine* will be safe.

(*There are boos.* **Bowler** *enters L.*)

(*aside*) Here is Bowler, my clerk. What the devil do you want?

**Bowler** Captain Noble, the gentleman who was here just now, wishes to see you again, Mr Snaker.

**Snaker** Tell him I've gone. Tell him . . .

(**Captain Noble** *bursts in L. He is a white-whiskered old seaman, though by his gestures he is more of an old actor.*)

**Noble** Give me back my money, my ten thousand pounds. Give it back, I say. You are a villain, a thief, a swindler.

(*There are cheers.*)

Give me my money. Five minutes after leaving your office I heard rumours that your credit had been shaken by the slump on Wall Street. Then I heard that — never mind what I heard. Enough that you would have taken my money and robbed my innocent children — my darling Percy, my sweet Lucy.

**Snaker**  But this is preposterous, sir! What money?

**Noble**  Ten thousand pounds in solid gold. You have it in that safe. I saw you place it there. I and your clerk here saw you. (*to* **Bowler**) Did you not? (*taking a paper from his pocket*) And here is your receipt.

(**Snaker** *looks anxious.*)

**Bowler**  (*snatching the receipt*) I saw nothing. I heard you speak of ten thousand pounds, but we get lots of crazy folk here.

**Noble**  Crazy! Merciful heavens! Crazy I shall be unless you ... (*He grabs vainly at the receipt.*)

**Bowler**  Crazy folks who babble about fortunes that don't exist. You go home quietly to your friends.

**Noble**  So you're in this swindle too, this conspiracy. (*He produces a pistol.*) Open that safe and give me my money, or I fire.

(*There are cheers.*)

**Snaker**  Seize him!

(**Bowler** *struggles with* **Noble** *and wrests the pistol from him.* **Snaker** *remains calm, twisting his moustachios in cynical indifference.*)

Now, after this exhibition, will you kindly go, or shall I call the police?

**Noble**  The pol —— (*He struggles from* **Bowler***'s grasp.*) You infernal pair of swindlers. I ... (*He is overcome by emtion and falls dead.*)

**Bowler**  (*stooping over* **Noble** *and feeling his heart*) Dead!

(*There are boos.*)

**Snaker**  Good! Now, Bowler, do as I tell you. Outside there is a thick fog. We must deposit the body where it will be found in due course. There is nothing about it to contradict the obvious surmise that this man died a perfectly natural death.

**Bowler**   And then?

**Snaker**   I don't understand you.

**Bowler**   What do you take me for? What do I get out of this?

**Snaker**   Do this and keep your mouth shut, and I will give you — five pounds.

**Bowler**   Five pounds! Five thousand pounds! Half-shares and no monkey tricks.

**Snaker**   You are mad.

**Bowler**   Mad! Don't forget I hold all the cards. Only I know about the fortune in that safe. Think of the story I can tell the police. I have the receipt ——

**Snaker**   Aha!

**Bowler**   — and the pistol. (*He produces the pistol.*) Hand over half the money, or . . .

**Snaker**   Foiled! Curse it!

(*There are cheers.*)

(*He goes slowly to the safe and takes out a bag of gold.*) Take one thousand.

**Bowler**  Five thousand.

**Snaker**  Take one thousand and spare me. Think of my innocent child.

**Bowler**  Think of Noble's receipt. Count yourself lucky that I do not demand the whole ten thousand. Think of the receipt. With this I could weave rope that will ... (*Still keeping* **Snaker** *covered, he makes a significant gesture.*)

**Snaker**  Foiled again! Curse you, curse you, curse you! (*pleading*) Do not be hard on a poor man. Think of my darling Alice, my only, my sweet, my innocent child.

**Bowler**  Quick. The money, or I take the receipt and vanish.

**Snaker**  Foiled again! Very well —— (*He opens the safe and flings five money bags on the desk.*) Keep your paltry scrap of paper, and much good may it do you. (*aside*) I will find a means yet to thwart him.

(*There are boos.*)

**Bowler**  (*putting the money bags into the portmanteau*) And now farewell, Silas Snaker. We shall meet again.
(*Still keeping* **Snaker** *covered, he goes to the door L.*)

**Snaker**  But, Bowler, what about the body?

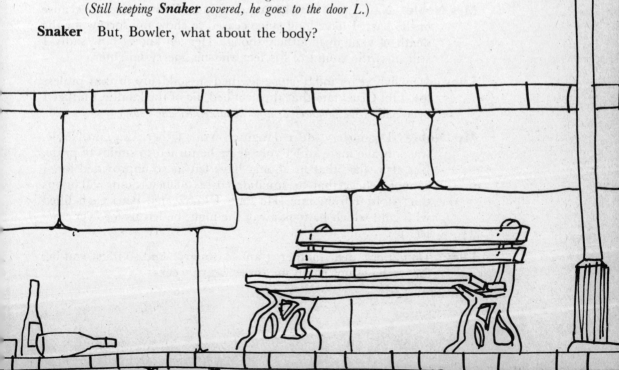

**Bowler**  Oh, I don't want it. Do what you like with it. Tip it out of the window. Lock it up in the safe. It's no use to me. Faaaaaaaaaaaaarewelllllllllllll!

(*Bowler exits L.*)

**Snaker**  Foiled again!

(*There are prolonged boos and hisses.*)


## SCENE 2

*The Thames Embankment. This scene can be played in front of a backcloth or curtains. There is a bench L and a bench R.*

*When the curtain rises the stage is in darkness except for spotlights on the two benches. Tragical music is played. Big Ben chimes; the wind blows, and snow falls. On the R bench* **Mrs Noble** *and* **Lucy** *sit clasped in each other's arms. On the L bench* **Bowler** *is huddled up asleep.* **Mrs Noble** *is weeping.*

**Lucy**  Do not cry, dear mother. (*She produces a handkerchief.*) Come, wipe your unhappy eyes that gaze so sadly on the past.

**Mrs Noble**  Nay, Lucy, my darling daughter, I do not weep because of the past. I have long since ceased to show my sorrow for the death of your dear father, though Heaven knows how sadly I still miss the sound of his feet and his merry laughter.

**Lucy**  It is five years today since he died so suddenly in that pitiless fog. Oh! Cruel fate that thus robbed me of the kindliest father I ever had. (*She produces another handkerchief and sobs.*)

**Mrs Noble**  Do not cry, dear daughter. Your father, Captain Noble, was a brave man, so let your tears be turned to smiles of pride. But alas, alas, that he should have left us so unprovided for. I cannot believe that he squandered his money. Some villainous thief stole it from him. He had, I know, ten bags each filled with gold which he took away the night he left us for ever. (*She sobs.*)

**Lucy**  Do not cry, dear mother. I am so hungry. And so must you be, for we have not eaten for three weary weeks.

**Mrs Noble**  Patience, darling, patience. Your brother, Percy, will be here at any moment. He is walking the streets in search of food.

**Lucy**  Ah, my brave and handsome brother, how I long to help him. Mother, why will you not let me help him?

**Mrs Noble**  (*rising*) Hush, hush, my child. (*aside*) She is so innocent. You may walk a few steps to see if he is coming, but do not go out of sight. I want you at my side.

**Lucy**  (*rising and looking L*) Mother, darling, here is Percy returning. Alas, his hands are empty. But stay, he has a companion. Saved! Saved! Percy has found a friend to help us in our destitution.

(*There are cheers. Music is played as **Percy** and **Harold** enter L.*)

**Percy**  Mother! Lucy! See whom I have found. Harold Headingford!

**Mrs Noble and Lucy**  (*together*) Harold Headingford!

(***Harold** advances to them. He is dressed in a sailor's jersey and trousers which do not quite meet. He frequently tries to cover the gap by violent tugs and hoists.*)

**Harold**  Yes, indeed, Mrs Noble, and sweet Lucy, it is I. We have not met since I ran away to sea ten years ago this very day.

**Lucy**  My brave Harold. (*She embraces **Harold** in a passionate, theatrical way.*)

**Harold**  My dear Lucy! So you still remember me.

**Lucy**  Yes, and I remember, too, the sacred vows of love we plighted in those happy childhood days.

**Harold**  I have been constant.

**Lucy**  And so have I. Now kindly fate has reunited us for ever.

(*They embrace again.*)

**Mrs Noble**  Alas that you should find us in such a miserable state, for we are penniless and starving, with scarce a roof above our heads. (*She sobs.*)

**Percy and Lucy**  (*together*) Do not cry, dear mother.

**Percy**   I have acquainted Harold with the sad history of our family misfortunes. Alas! His own tale is no less pitiful. But stay. Rest awhile on this bench and he shall tell you.

(**Lucy** and **Mrs Noble** *sit.*)

We have but scant provender for you, but shortly Harold and I will search again. (*He takes a chestnut from his pocket.*) Take this, mother, it was all I could secure — a roasted chestnut. I fear it is a little cold by now.

**Harold**   (*also taking a chestnut from his pocket*) Sweet Lucy, I also procured one which you must have.

**Mrs Noble and Lucy**   (*together*) No, no, I cannot eat it all. You must share.

(*The chestnuts are divided.* **Harold** *and* **Percy** *sit at the feet of the women. They all nibble hungrily.*)

**Percy**   (*starting up; aside*) Soft! Who is the poor fellow yonder? He, too, looks cold and hungry. He shall share my frugal meal. I cannot eat when I behold such suffering. (*He crosses to* **Bowler** *and awakens him.*) Sir, sir, I cannot doubt but that you are in some distress. I, too, am penniless and starving, but I can at least offer you the comfort of half of my half-chestnut.

**Bowler**   Heaven bless you for your kind words. It is true; I am starving. Once I had wealth — no matter how I got it — but I was foolish and gambled my fortune away. Your kindness gives me fresh hope.

(**Bowler** *and* **Percy** *eat and converse.*)

**Mrs Noble**   (*to* **Harold**) So your plight is even worse than ours? No roof to shelter you. Alas, that we should know such sorrow. (*She sobs.*)

**Lucy**   Do not cry, dear mother. Harold shall come home with us to our mean attic. I would like to have him there.

**Mrs Noble**   Hush, hush, my child. (*aside*) She is so innocent.

**Bowler**   (*to* **Percy**) And once I find this gentleman, I shall make him pay. I have a certain slip of paper that he will gladly buy for ten thousand pounds.

**Percy**  Heavens! Is there so much money in the world?

**Bowler**  You are young and money is a god to children. But hear me, my lad, an easy conscience and a contented heart are worth all the gold in the world.

**Percy**  Thank you. Now I must go, but first tell me your name.

**Bowler**  My name is Bowler. And yours?

**Percy**  Percy Noble, son of the late Captain Noble.

**Bowler**  (*aside*) Merciful Heaven. Can this be possible?

**Percy**  And yonder are my starving mother and sister whom I must rejoin. Good-bye, Mr Bowler, and may Heaven bless you. (*He rejoins the others.*) Come, let us go. Harold and I to the Opera House where we may perchance earn a copper or two by holding the horses' heads. You, my dear mother and sweet Lucy, go back to our mean attic in Cross Keys Street, and we will join you within the hour.

(**Mrs Noble** *sobs.*)

**Percy and Lucy**  (*together*) Do not cry, dear mother.

(*They kiss and depart.* **Harold** *and* **Percy** *exit L.* **Mrs Noble** *and* **Lucy** *exit R.*)

**Bowler**  (*rising*) Poor, poor, poor people. How my heart bleeds for them. How brave and kind they are. (*He advances downstage.*) Now I am resolved. That villainous thief, Silas Snaker, shall pay for this. I will renew my weary search for him and force him to pay me the money which I will then hand over to Percy Noble. The vile and rascally Snaker must not, *shall* not, rob these poor and innocent gentlefolk.

(*There are cheers.*)

(*He looks off L.*) But soft, do my eyes deceive me? It cannot be ... But yes it is — none other than Snaker himself coming this way, doubtless from some sumptuous banquet. Thank you, O Heaven, for thus delivering the villain into my hands.

(*Sinister music is played as* **Snaker**, *in astrakhan, enters L. He carries a stick. There are boos.*)

A word with you, if you please.

**Snaker**  Out of my way, cur. I have no pity for beggars.

**Bowler**  I do not beg. I demand.

**Snaker**  (*raising his stick*) Insolent dog. Who are you?

**Bowler**  My name is Bowler. I was once your clerk.

**Snaker**  (*aside*) That name strikes terror in my heart. Bowler? Ah! Yes, I believe I did once employ a fellow of that name. But I have no need for clerks now. Here, take this shilling and let me pass.

**Bowler**  No, no, my fine sir!

**Snaker**  (*aside*) Foiled!

**Bowler**  For three years I have searched for you high and low. Now fate has brought us together.

**Snaker**  I do not understand you. Be brief or let me pass.

**Bowler**  Noble! Ten thousand pounds! Receipt! Do those words strike any answering chord in your black heart? Aha, I see they do. I still have that receipt. Unless you pay me ten thousand pounds I will go straight to the police!

**Snaker**  (*aside*) Foiled again! Let me see this receipt. (*aside*) He may have lost it.

**Bowler**  Ha! Ha! It is too precious to carry about. I have it in my lodgings, and you must come for it and bring the money with you.

**Snaker**  (*aside*) Curse him, he has me in his power. Yet I may still find a way to thwart him. Very well, I will visit you tomorrow.

**Bowler**  Within the hour you must come or your vile secret will be with the police. I live in Cross Keys Street. My lodgings are but a mean attic, but you will find me waiting. Farewell, Silas Snaker, and on your peril, fail me not.

(***Bowler*** *exits R.*)

**Snaker**  Foiled again.

(***Snaker*** *exits L.*)

## SCENE 3

*The Attics in Cross Keys Street. The stage is divided into two attics, with a short length of party wall between them. The room R belongs to* ***Bowler*** *and the room L to* ***Mrs Noble***. *Each room has a door and a window. In the room R are a small camp-bed, table, chair and a cupboard; in the room L a table and two chairs.*

*When the curtain rises* ***Mrs Noble*** *and* ***Lucy*** *are discovered sitting in the chairs.*

**Lucy**  Surely an hour has passed, and Percy and Harold have not yet returned.

**Mrs Noble**  Oh! Merciful Father! Protect my innocent children.

(***Bowler*** *enters his room R.*)

**Bowler**  Back again to these miserable lodgings. How dark it is. (*He takes a box containing two matches, from his pocket.*) I have but two matches left, but what matter — (*lighting the candle*) — this poor candle must be both light and heat for me for I have no fuel at all.

**Lucy**  Do not cry, dear mother. See, the candle is going out.

**Mrs Noble**  So much the better. Now you will not be able to see my tears.

**Bowler**  (*going to the cupboard*) What poor provisions have I left? Tonight I will eat all that is left, for surely Percy Noble will no longer let me starve once I have retrieved his family fortune.

**Lucy**  (*aside*) Is there no way to end this misery? None but death!

**Bowler**    (*examining a bottle*) Ha, ha! One last bottle of honest ale remains. This shall warm me and cheer me up for my encounter with the rascally Snaker. A few dry crusts and this piece of raw meat I snatched from a dog last week, these must perforce be my repast. (*He sits and proceeds to roast the meat over the candle.*)

**Mrs Noble**    (*aside*) If Percy had only Lucy to support, they might live. Why should I prolong my life merely to shorten theirs?

**Bowler**    (*rising and examining the party wall*) This room grows draughtier than ever. What can it be? Why, yes, there are great chinks in the wall here. Heaven grant that I may soon be free of the place and live once more in the comfort I used to know. A new family moved in next door some days ago. I have not seen them. I wonder who they are? (*He resumes his meal.*)

**Lucy**    (*aside*) There is but one solution: I must die. When I am gone there will be one less mouth to feed. My duty is plain: I must think of my mother. My sacrifice is for her alone.

**Mrs Noble**    (*aside*) In this room there is some charcoal. (*She rises.*) But is there enough to bestow on me an easy death?

(**Mrs Noble** *exits.*)

**Lucy**    What is mother doing? (*She looks through the door.*) She is lighting the pan of charcoal on which we prepare our food. Ah! A thought! Could I induce her to leave me alone, the deadly fumes of the fuel would soon bestow on me an easy death.

(**Mrs Noble** *enters.*)

**Mrs Noble**    (*aside*) It is there; now while I have the courage of despair.

**Bowler**    Snaker should soon be here. What is the time, I wonder?

(*A church clock strikes ten very erratically.*)

Ha! Ten o'clock.

(*The clock strikes once more.*)

Eleven o'clock. He will be here anon I have no doubt.

**Lucy**  Dear mother, I have just thought of a friend, a working girl, from whom I might beg a crust.

**Mrs Noble**  Go then, my child — go at once.

**Lucy**  I fear to go alone. Come with me and wait at the corner of the street till I come out.

**Mrs Noble**  (*aside*) When she is out of sight I can return and accomplish my purpose.

**Lucy**  (*aside*) I will leave her and come back quickly by another way to accomplish my purpose.

**Mrs Noble**  Come, Lucy. (*She sobs.*)

**Lucy**  (*as they go to the door*) Do not cry, dear mother.

(**Mrs Noble** *and* **Lucy** *exit.*)

**Bowler**  (*draining the bottle*) Gone, all is gone. But now I must make ready for my guest. Ha! Ha! (*He clears the table.*)

(*Horses' hooves are heard offstage.*)

He comes! I hear his carriage below. The receipt! (*He opens the cupboard.*) Yes, safely here. (*He puts it in his pocket.*) Now I am ready to bargain with this vile monster.

(*Music is heard as* **Snaker** *enters R.*)

**Snaker**  Ah! ha! So this is your abode? (*aside*) This place fills me with horror and foreboding. I must get the receipt and go quickly. Where is the receipt you spoke of?

**Bowler**  Not so fast. Where is the money I also spoke of?

**Snaker**  I have left it below guarded by my coachman. You shall have it when you have given me the receipt — *if* you have got the receipt, which I greatly doubt.

**Bowler**  Make no mistake, the receipt is here in my pocket.

**Snaker**  You lie.

**Bowler**  (*producing the receipt*) There! Vile wretch. It is you who lie.

**Snaker**   (*chasing* **Bowler** *round the table*) Give it to me. Curse you, curse you, curse you.

**Bowler**   Not so fast. Bring me the money and it is yours.

**Snaker**   (*producing a pistol*) Give it to me at once, or I'll blow your brains out.

**Bowler**   So that is your calculation.

**Snaker**   Now I have you in my power. Ha! ha! ha! I am one too many for you.

**Bowler**   (*producing two pistols from under the bed*) And I am one too many for you. I defy you, Silas Snaker.

(*There are cheers.*)

**Snaker**   (*dropping the pistol; aside*) Damnation! Foiled again. Curse him, I am at his mercy. Ha! ha! ha! I was merely playing. I hope my little joke didn't upset you.

**Bowler**   A joke you say? Very well, you shall pay for your joke. It will cost you an extra thousand pounds. Unless you bring to me within fifteen minutes the sum of eleven thousand pounds I shall go straight to the police.

**Snaker**   Mercy! Mercy! I shall be ruined.

**Bowler**   Perhaps you would rather be hanged?

**Snaker**   No! no! Anything but that. Give me time to pay. Here, take my purse and I will visit you again next week.

**Bowler**   Your purse is too small for my liking. Go, fetch the full amount within fifteen minutes or I will expose your villainy to the whole world. Go!

**Snaker**   (*going to the door and turning*) Foiled again.

(**Snaker** *exits. There are boos.*)

**Bowler**   So! Now I can take my ease for a few minutes. (*He sits.*)

(**Lucy** *enters L.*)

**Lucy**   I took a shortcut and ran home. Now I am alone, the fumes of charcoal shall fill this little room and send me to sleep for ever. I must fetch the pan. (*She exits.*)

**Bowler**   Ah, how I look forward to relieving the widow and her fatherless children.

(*Mrs Noble* enters L.)

**Mrs Noble**  Poor Lucy. I dared not look back at her as we parted for ever. Despair hastened my steps. My poor, innocent children. I have given you all I had, and now I hope my wretched life will serve you in your terrible need.

**Bowler**  (*sniffing*) I smell charcoal, burning charcoal. (*He rises.*) Where can it be coming from? I have a queer feeling in my head. Let me lie down awhile. (*He lies on the bed.*)

(*Lucy* enters L with a charcoal brazier.)

**Lucy**  The moment has arrived.

**Mrs Noble**  (*seeing her*) Lucy!

**Lucy**  Mother!

**Mrs Noble**  My child, what is this? For what purpose are you here?

**Lucy**  You, too, mother? Like me, you wished to die?

**Mrs Noble**  No! no! You shall not die! My darling child, you are too young. Life is before you — hope — happiness. (*She sobs.*)

**Lucy**  Do not cry, dear mother. Is it not better to die like this than by either grief or hunger?

**Mrs Noble**  (*falling into a chair*) Already my senses fail me. Lucy, my child, live, live!

**Lucy**  No! No, dear mother, let us die together. First I must lock the door. (*She locks the door and then kneels beside her mother.*) Let us pray together for those whom we leave. Can you hear me, mother?

**Bowler**  Oh! I feel so ill. Why does my brain reel so; why does my head throb? (*He groans.*)

(*There is a knocking on the door L. **Percy** and **Harold** are outside.*)

**Percy**  (*off*) The door is locked, Harold. What can it mean? Mother, Lucy, open the door. It is I, Percy. What is wrong? Mother, we have food for you. Open! Open!

(*Lucy* falls prostrate.)

Harold, help me to burst open the door.

(**Harold** and **Percy** *burst open the door and enter.*)

Woe is me! What is this? They have committed suicide.

(**Percy** *rushes to* **Mrs Noble** *and* **Harold** *to* **Lucy**. *They take out handkerchiefs and fan the women vigorously.*)

**Bowler** (*rising*) I cannot breathe. Oh! Heaven, why do you torture me thus. I am dying — dying within a moment of triumph. (*He chokes.*) I am suffocating. What can I do? I cannot see. Oh! how my head spins.

(**Mrs Noble** *and* **Lucy** *revive.*)

**Percy** There, there, dear mother, all is well. The fresh air has revived you. Thank Heaven we were in time.

**Mrs Noble** My brave boy, you have rescued us from the grave. I had planned it all for your sake.

**Bowler** Justice of Heaven! I am strangling — (*tearing off his collar*) — and Snaker will be here at any moment. If he finds me thus he will rob me of my receipt just as he robbed that poor old sailor. I know him of old. I must get help. (*He knocks on the party wall.*) Help, help, good neighbours.

(**Snaker** *enters R carrying a portmanteau.* **Bowler** *falls unconscious.*)

**Percy** What was that? I heard a muffled cry for help.

**Harold** And so did I. It seemed to come from the next room.

**Lucy** Let us go and see if we can render assistance.

(*They all exit.*)

**Snaker** Ah, ha! So he is drunk. Now I have him in my power. But how stifling it is in here. I must open the window or I shall choke. (*He opens the window.*) Poor fool, how he has played into my hands. (*He kicks* **Bowler**.) Take that, and that, and that. Now for the receipt. Which pocket did he use? (*He kneels by* **Bowler**.)

(**Mrs Noble**, **Lucy**, **Percy** *and* **Harold** *enter R.*)

**Percy**   Pardon us, sir, but we heard a cry for help and have come to render assistance.

**Snaker**   (*rising; aside*) Foiled again! Ah, my friends, this is good of you, but there is nothing you can do. My friend has merely swooned, but I am a doctor and I will take care of him myself. Thank you most kindly. Good night!

**Harold**   But is there nothing we can do? He looks so ill and there is blood on his forehead.

**Snaker**   (*aside*) Curse it, that is where I kicked him. No, no, my friends, you may safely leave him to me. Good night!

**Mrs Noble**   Nay, I will fetch some water for his poor bruised lips.

**Snaker**   (*aside*) Curse it! My second kick. I can attend to all. Good night.

**Lucy**   Here, take my handkerchief to bind his bloody neck.

**Mrs Noble**   Hush, hush, my child. (*aside*) She is so innocent.

(**Bowler** *revives.*)

**Bowler**   (*sitting up*) Where am I?

**All**   Ah! He is coming to.

**Snaker**   And so, my friends, I bid you good night. (*He starts to shepherd them out.*)

**Bowler**   (*rising*) Stay! Do not go. And, most important, do not let him go. He is a thief, nay, little better than a murderer.

(*There are cheers.*)

**Snaker**   (*aside*) Foiled again!

**Percy**   Why! Mr Bowler!

**Bowler**   By all that's wonderful — Percy Noble.

**Snaker**   (*aside*) Noble! That name again. I fear the worst is about to befall me.

**Percy**   Let me introduce my mother and my sister Lucy. This is a poor friend whom I met tonight.

(*They all bow.*)

**Bowler**  (*aside*) How charming and gracious the old lady is. I believe I love her.

**Mrs Noble**  (*aside*) How unhappy he looks. Yet how brave and noble. I believe I love him.

**Bowler**  Mrs Noble, dear madam. As you and yours have so gallantly come to my aid, now may I help you and relieve you of your cares.

**Mrs Noble**  (*aside*) What *can* he mean? This is so sudden.

**Bowler**  Five years ago this very night your gallant husband met with sudden but natural death.

**Lucy and Percy**  (*together*) Do not cry, dear mother.

**Bowler**  Shortly before this cruel fate overtook him, he entrusted to Silas Snaker, a banker, ten bags of golden sovereigns. I was there, I saw it all.

**Lucy, Percy and Mrs Noble**  (*together*) You.

**Bowler**  Yes. I must confess, to my shame, that I helped the villain, Snaker, to embezzle the money. But that is past. I am reformed — won back to virtue by the kindliness of your noble son and the gentleness of your lovely face. I am ready to make amends with my life. Nay, more, I am about to restore your husband's savings into your hands.

**Mrs Noble**   Sir, I am amazed at what you tell us. How can this be?

**Bowler**   (*pointing to* **Snaker**) There stands the monstrous villain, Silas Snaker.

**Lucy, Percy and Mrs Noble**   (*together*) Vile, ignoble creature!

(*There are boos and hisses.*)

**Snaker**   (*aside*) Damnation and fury. Can I find a way out? My good friends, I have let this go too far and I must apologize. As I told you a few moments ago, I am a doctor, and this is my patient. So much is true. (*He points to the portmanteau.*) There is my professional bag. But when I said he swooned, I lied, merely to save your feelings. He was in a fit. He is subject to fits, dreadful fits in which he bites his lips and bangs his head. He is dangerous. In fact, my good friends, he is a lunatic, and I have traced him here to take him back to Colney Hatch. Now leave us at once while you are safe.

(*They all back to the door with suitable exclamations of horror.*)

**Bowler**   Stop! Do not believe this lying rogue. I have proof of my story.

**Snaker**   (*aside*) The receipt! Foiled again!

**Bowler**   (*taking the receipt from his pocket*) Here is the receipt signed by his own hand, and there in the bag is the money he stole.

**Percy**   (*examining both*) Mother, it is true! We are rich again.

**Mrs Noble**   Oh! Happy circumstance. Mr Bowler, how can I ever express my thanks? (*She offers her hand to* **Bowler**. *Bowler kisses her hand.*)

**Percy**   (*to* **Snaker**) And you, miserable miscreant, have you nothing to say before we send for the police?

**Snaker**   Alas, what can I say? I am undone, exposed, unmasked — and utterly foiled.

**Percy**   Is there not one thing in his favour?

**Snaker**   Nothing, save this. All I have done has been because of love

— love of my sweet, innocent and motherless daughter. For her alone I desired riches and high degree. For her alone I have striven these last five weary years. Sweet, darling Alice, I can see her now. (*He sobs.*)

**Lucy**   (*to **Snaker**; absent-mindedly*) Do not cry, dear mother.

**Mrs Noble**   My heart is touched. I have seen too much of suffering. Do not send him to gaol. Let him go.

**Bowler**   My sweet angel, your forgiving heart is a shining example to us all.

**Percy**   Be it so. Snaker, you may thank my mother for this generous clemency. Let her noble sacrifice be an example to you. Mend your ways, cleanse your heart, resolve to follow the path of virtue — and never darken my doors again.

**Snaker**   I am resolved. Henceforward I shall be an honourable and humble man. Nor pleasures nor palaces shall ever tempt me more.

**All**   Amen.

(***Snaker** exits to soft music.*)

**Harold**   And now, Lucy, I claim your hand.

**Bowler**   And I, sweet madam, humbly sue for yours.

**Mrs Noble and Lucy**   (*together*) We have learned the value of poverty. It opens the heart.

**Percy**   (*coming to the front of the stage and addressing the audience*) Is this true? Have the sufferings we have depicted opened your hearts and caused a sympathetic tear to fill your eyes? If so, extend to us your hands.

**Mrs Noble**   (*to the audience*) No, not to us. But when you leave this place, as you go home, should you see some poor creatures, extend your hands to them and Heaven will shower blessings in your way.

*CURTAIN*

## Production Notes

*Hiss the Villain!* is modelled very closely on the type of melodrama which was immensely popular in the 1850s. It should be played with great earnestness and sincerity, and the actors must never move outside their characters for the sake of a laugh. The Victorian audience played almost as large a part in the performance as the actors themselves, sharing very enthusiastically in the emotions of the hero and heroine. It is, therefore, essential to a really good performance to get your audience entering wholeheartedly into the fun. In the original performance a *claque* (a hired body of applauders) was enlisted. They attended several rehearsals and soon became proficient in hissing and cheering at appropriate moments. On the night of the performance the audience quickly 'cottoned-on' and the play went with a tremendous swing.

A good deal of extra fun can be devised with the snow in Scene 2 by selecting special moments and places for it to fall. For instance, a brief shower of scarlet snow at Bowler's line 'How my heart bleeds for them' always brings the house down. Again, an apparently involuntary snowfall in the middle of Scene 3 is very successful!

Lucy's oft-repeated 'Do not cry, dear mother' is more pointed if she produces each time a tiny handkerchief, and especially if they are all fresh handkerchiefs produced from unexpected quarters of her costume.

The costumes themselves present little difficulty. Snaker has a frock coat; Percy, a much-too-small Norfolk suit; and the ladies are shabbily genteel in long skirts and leg-o'-mutton sleeves.

Music can help the atmosphere immensely, especially the sentimental piece 'Hearts and Flowers', played softly at pathetic moments. A small orchestra is best, of course, but, failing that, a piano and violin, or even a gramophone, would be useful.

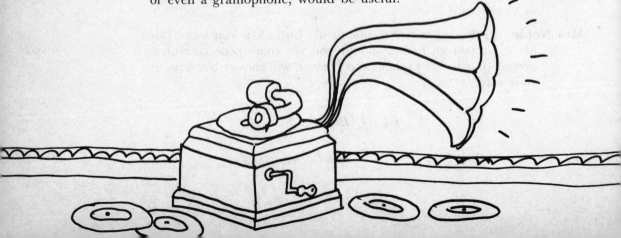

## Questions

1  In what way is Snaker an obvious villain?

2  What is his motto?

3  How is the audience encouraged to show its disapproval of the villain?

4  What reasons does Snaker give for robbing Captain Noble?

5  How does Snaker arrange the robbery?

6  What kind of emotion is the audience supposed to feel as Scene 2 opens?

7  How does Snaker, who is returning from a sumptuous banquet, treat the poverty-stricken Bowler?

8  What causes Snaker to say, about Bowler, 'Curse him, he has me in his power'?

9  Why does Mrs Noble contemplate suicide?

10  Why does Lucy contemplate suicide?

11  In what simple way does Bowler get the upper hand when Snaker pulls a pistol on him?

12  *Snaker:* Ah, ha! So he is drunk. Now I have him in my power.
What has really happened to Bowler?

13  Snaker is disturbed as he attacks Bowler. Who does he try to pass himself off as?

14  '*They all back to the door with suitable exclamations of horror.*' What has Snaker just said to them to cause this?

15  Explain how a happy ending is arranged for everyone as the play closes.

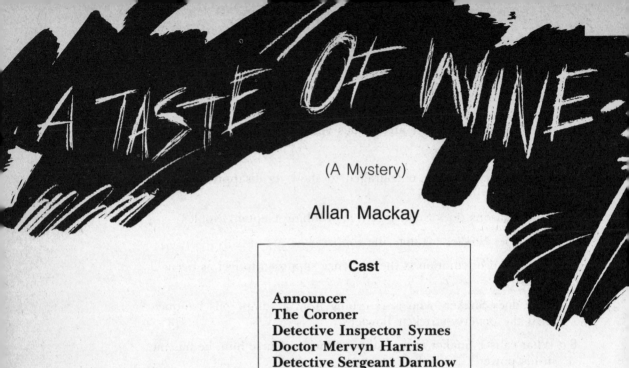

# A TASTE OF WINE

(A Mystery)

## Allan Mackay

**Cast**

**Announcer**
**The Coroner**
**Detective Inspector Symes**
**Doctor Mervyn Harris**
**Detective Sergeant Darnlow**
**James Fitzgerald**
**Eric Langdon**
**Susan Langdon**
**Neil Langdon**
**Doctor Richard Edgar**

## Introduction

This drama is an attempt to blend the tense atmosphere of a courtroom inquiry and the mystery of an unsolved murder. To increase the tension further, the events of the case have been telescoped into about thirty minutes, in which the crime is described, investigated and, it is hoped, solved. Because the aim is tension and the challenge is to the mind rather than to the senses, the important thing is pace. Most of the exchanges are brief and quick so that, except for the interruptions of the Announcer, a fast pace is kept up throughout. This is not to say that the actors should speak quickly, but rather that they should anticipate their cues and speak without hesitation. It is essential, of course, that the play be acted straight through without a break.

The play is a challenge to the audience to solve the mystery. It also tries to involve them, in the form of a jury weighing the evidence. The producer must, therefore, stress the importance of absolute silence throughout the performance. The time for discussion and decision comes at the end.

## SCENE

*A courtroom. A raised judge's bench with a chair behind, midstage, facing out. Seated here is the* **Coroner**. *To the right is the witness-box. To the left is a long row of chairs, facing out at an angle to the audience. On these are seated the other characters listed above, except the* **Announcer** *and* **Symes**. *The latter is standing beside the witness-box, consulting his notes.*

*The* **Announcer** *enters and walks to the front. He remains there, to one side, during the play.*

**Announcer** Ladies and gentlemen of the audience, what you are about to see is not a trial. It is the Coroner's inquiry into the sudden death of Sir Henry Langdon. It is to be conducted by the Coroner with the assistance of Detective Inspector Symes who had charge of the case. Those people seated in front there will give evidence in this affair.

This inquiry has ben made necessary by the failure of the police to solve the case. Only one fact seemed certain: that Sir Henry was murdered by one of three people, his children, who were with him when he died. But which one? All three stood to gain by his death, so it is not a question of motive. What is more, they all had the opportunity. But Sir Henry died in an odd and mysterious way and it was here that the police were baffled. Just how *did* he die? So you see, the Coroner's task is a difficult one. At the end of the inquiry he must present one of two verdicts: death by a named person or death by hands unknown.

Sir Henry Langdon was one of the most famous men in the country. He was also one of the richest. He had been retired for several years, ever since arthritis had confined him to a wheelchair. At the time of his death, he lived alone in his large house outside the city of Casewell. Sir Henry was at best a very

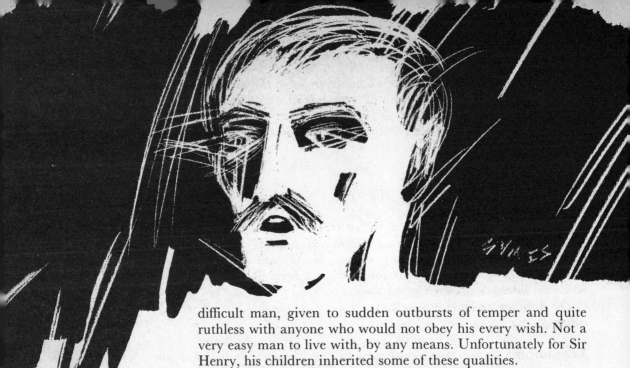

difficult man, given to sudden outbursts of temper and quite ruthless with anyone who would not obey his every wish. Not a very easy man to live with, by any means. Unfortunately for Sir Henry, his children inherited some of these qualities.

Ladies and gentlemen, I want you to play an important part in this inquiry. Someone killed Sir Henry; but who was it and how was it done? Though the final decision must come from the Coroner, I want you to help him, to act as a sort of jury and deliver your verdict. But whatever you do, save your verdict until it is all over. Then consider your findings carefully.

An official inquiry is a long business, so we have cut it down to only those facts that are important and to the few people who are essential to the case.

Now, to begin. At about eight p.m. on the night of August 5th, Sir Henry Langdon died in the dining room of his house. With him when he died were his three children, Susan, Eric and Neil.

**Coroner**  Inspector Symes, are you ready to begin?

**Symes**  Yes, Mr Coroner. All the witnesses are present.

**Coroner**  Very well. Proceed.

**Symes**  I call Doctor Mervyn Harris.

(**Doctor Harris** *rises and goes to the witness-box.*)

**Announcer**  Mervyn Harris, aged sixty-one, lives and works in Casewell. He had been Sir Henry's doctor for many years.

**Symes**  Doctor Harris, on the night of August the 5th, you received phone call from Eric Langdon?

**Harris**  I did.

**Symes**  What time was that?

**Harris**  A few minutes after eight.

**Symes**  Where was he calling from?

**Harris**  Sir Henry's house.

**Symes**  What was the call about?

**Harris**  Henry Langdon had died.

**Symes**  Did you go out there?

**Harris**  Yes. I arrived there about eight-thirty.

**Symes**  And you examined the body?

**Harris**  Only briefly.

**Symes**  How long had Mr Langdon been dead?

**Harris**  As far as I could tell, about thirty minutes.

**Symes**  Where was the body?

**Harris**  Slumped in a wheelchair at the dinner table.

**Coroner**  Could you be a little more exact, Doctor?

**Harris**  Henry was lying against the back of the chair. Obvious attempts had been made to revive him — his collar was loosened. He still had his wine glass in his hand.

**Coroner**  Doesn't that seem a bit strange, Doctor — the wine glass, I mean?

**Harris**  Not really. In his struggle to breathe, Henry must have clutched it tightly. His fingers were clamped around the stem.

**Coroner**  Then at any time it would have been difficult to take the glass from him — to exchange it, perhaps, for another glass?

**Harris**  Almost impossible.

**Coroner**  Thank you. Continue, Mr Symes.

**Symes**  Could you tell what had caused Sir Henry's death, Doctor?

**Harris**  Certainly — poison. Arsenic, I believe.

**Symes**  Why arsenic?

**Harris**  I could smell it on sir Henry's lips.

**Symes**  Not in the wine?

**Harris**  I didn't test the wine.

**Symes**  What did you do after you had examined the body?

**Harris**  I suggested they call the police.

**Symes**  They?

**Harris**  Susan, Eric and Neil Langdon. They were in the room when I arrived.

**Symes**  Why did you suggest the police?

**Harris**  I believed Henry had been murdered.

**Symes**  Did you dismiss suicide, Doctor?

**Harris**   Oh, yes! Henry wasn't the type.

**Symes**   He *was* confined to a wheelchair, wasn't he?

**Harris**   Yes — for arthritis. But Henry never let his sickness beat him.

**Symes**   Did you remain in the room until the police arrived?

**Harris**   I did.

**Symes**   Did you move anything — on the table, for instance?

**Harris**   No.

**Symes**   Did any of the three children touch anything?

**Harris**   No. They went into the next room.

**Symes**   Thank you, Doctor.

**Coroner**   Doctor Harris, did you know Sir Henry's children well?

**Harris**   Yes — until they left home.

**Coroner**   Why did they leave?

**Harris**   Henry told me he quarrelled with them.

**Coroner**   All three?

**Harris**   Yes — but not all at the same time.

**Coroner**   What did they quarrel about?

**Harris**   I'm not sure. I think it had something to do with Henry wanting to manage their lives. One thing he did say over and over again though....

**Coroner**   Yes?

**Harris**   They all hated him.

**Coroner**   Thank you, Doctor, you may step down.

> (***Doctor Harris*** *returns to his seat.*)

**Symes**   I call Detective Sergeant Robert Darnlow.

> (***Darnlow*** *rises and goes to the witness-box.*)

**Announcer**   Detective Sergeant Darnlow is stationed in Casewell. He carried out most of the inquiries into Sir Henry's death and was the first policeman on the scene.

**Symes**   Mr Darnlow, you were called to Henry Langdon's house on the night of August the 5th?

**Darnlow**   I was. Doctor Harris called me.

**Symes**   What time did you arrive?

**Darnlow**   About nine-fifteen.

**Symes**   Was the scene as Doctor Harris described it?

**Darnlow**   Yes.

**Symes**   Did you search the house?

**Darnlow**   My men did.

**Symes**   Did you find any poison?

**Darnlow**   Not in the house. But in the gardener's shed we found a packet of rat poison. It's mostly arsenic.

**Symes**  Was the packet open?

**Darnlow**  It was — and there was some missing.

**Symes**  What did you do then?

**Darnlow**  I called forensic to examine the dining room.

**Symes**  Concentrating now on the glass in Sir Henry's hand, did you find any fingerprints on it?

**Darnlow**  I did. Two sets: Sir Henry's and Susan Langdon's.

(*Susan Langdon* jumps to her feet.)

**Susan**  Of course mine were there! I gave him the glass. . . .

(*She realizes what she has said and sits down slowly.*)

**Coroner**  Miss Langdon, I must ask you not to interrupt. Go on, Mister Darnlow.

**Darnlow**  Well, I took the three of them into Casewell for further questioning.

**Symes**  What has been the result of police inquiries into the crime?

**Darnlow**  Only the conclusion that Henry Langdon *was* murdered — and by one of his three children.

**Symes**  Why do you say that?

**Darnlow**  They were the only ones in the house at the time. And they all stood to gain from his death.

**Symes**  Thank you, Mr Darnlow. You may step down.

(*Darnlow* returns to his seat.)

I call James Fitzgerald.

(*James Fitzgerald* rises and goes to the witness-box.)

**Announcer**  James Fitzgerald, solicitor, had charge of all Henry Langdon's business affairs. He was also a personal friend of the dead man.

**Symes**  Mr Fitzgerald, please describe your dealings with Henry Langdon in the days leading to his death.

**Fitzgerald**   Several days before he died, Henry called on me to tell me he intended changing his will.

**Symes**   Was he a wealthy man?

**Fitzgerald**   Very.

**Symes**   What were the contents of his original will?

**Fitzgerald**   All his wealth was to be divided among his children.

**Symes**   And the new will?

**Fitzgerald**   We drew it up the day before he died. Most of his wealth was to go into medical research into arthritis. The children received small grants.

**Symes**   Was the new will signed?

**Fitzgerald**   No. Henry died before —

**Symes**   Yes, I see. Why did Henry Langdon decide to change his will?

**Fitzgerald**   He hated his sickness and ... (*He hesitates.*)

**Symes**   Go on, Mr Fitzgerald.

**Fitzgerald**   He was disgusted with his children.

**Symes**   Why?

**Fitzgerald**   They refused to have anything to do with him. They never called to see him.

**Symes**   But they came home the morning of his death?

**Fitzgerald**   Oh, yes. He called them and told them he was changing his will.

**Symes**   Why did he do that?

**Fitzgerald**   I think Henry was trying to make a point.

**Symes**   What point was that?

**Fitzgerald**   That it was only money that would bring his children home.

**Symes**   Thank you, Mr Fitzgerald.

**Coroner**   Mr Fitzgerald, in your opinion, did the Langdon children hate their father?

**Fitzgerald**   Hate is a bit strong. Let's just say they didn't particularly like him.

**Coroner**   Can you give any reason for this?

**Fitzgerald**   At times Henry could be a cruel man, a man without pity. He expected his children to obey his every wish.

**Coroner**   Then you blame Sir Henry?

**Fitzgerald**   Not completely. He was hard but his children had everything they wanted — except perhaps love.

**Coroner**   Thank you. You may step down.

(***Fitzgerald*** *returns to his seat.*)

**Symes**  I call Eric Langdon.

(*Eric Langdon* rises and goes to the witness-box.)

**Announcer**  Eric Langdon at thirty-one is the eldest of the Langdon children.

**Symes**  Mr Langdon, will you please tell us what happened on the day your father died.

**Eric**  That morning my father had telephoned me to tell me that he was going to change his will —

**Symes**  Did you know the contents of the first will?

**Eric**  We all did. My father kept no secrets where money was concerned.

**Symes**  And you were upset about the new one?

**Eric**  I was — angry, I suppose. It wasn't fair.

**Symes**  Fair? We have heard that you wouldn't have anything to do with your father.

**Eric**  That was his fault, not mine. *He* was impossible to live with, not me.

**Symes**  Go on, Mr Langdon.

**Eric**  I drove over later that morning.

**Symes**  Why?

**Eric**  I suppose I hoped to change his mind. In any case, father expected it. It was all part of the game.

**Symes**  Did you all arrive together?

**Eric**  No. Susan arrived by car a little later. Neil came by train.

**Symes**  Did you change your father's mind?

**Eric**  No. We kept at him all afternoon, but he wouldn't budge. I think ... he was enjoying himself.

**Symes**  I see. Go on.

**Eric**  Well, about half-past four, father went to his room to rest.

**Symes**  What did you and your brother and sister do?

**Eric**  Susan drove into town. Neil went to the library to read....

**Symes**  And you, Mr Langdon?

**Eric**  I went for a walk.

**Symes**  In the garden?

**Eric**  Yes.

**Symes**  Speak up, Mr Langdon. Did you go to the gardener's shed?

**Eric**  No!

**Symes**  You're a chemist, aren't you, Mr Langdon?

**Eric**  Yes.

**Symes**  Then you would easily recognize arsenic, wouldn't you?

**Eric**  Yes, but anyone —

**Coroner**  Come, come, Mr Symes, that's hardly a fair question.

**Symes**  I'm sorry, Mr Coroner. Mr Langdon, when did you next see your father?

**Eric**  About seven — at dinner.

**Symes**  Who cooked the meal?

**Eric**  Susan. Father had asked her earlier.

**Symes**  Go on.

**Eric**  After the meal we all stayed at the table, talking about the will. At least father was talking. We had given up hope of changing his mind.

**Symes**  Describe your places at the table, please.

**Eric**  Susan sat on father's left, Neil on his right. I sat opposite.

**Symes**  How wide is the table?

**Eric**  About three feet.

**Symes**  Then you could easily reach your father?

**Eric**  We all could!

**Symes**  What happened then?

**Eric**  Father asked Susan to get some wine.

**Symes**  Where was the wine?

**Eric**  On the sideboard with the glasses.

**Symes**  Where did Susan pour the wine?

**Eric**  At the sideboard.

**Symes**  Did she have her back to the table?

**Eric**  Yes . . . I think so. (*He stares at* **Susan.**)

**Symes**  Did you watch her pouring it?

**Eric**  No . . . Susan, you —

**Susan**   No, no Eric — I didn't —

**Coroner**   Miss Langdon, please make no comment until you are in the witness-box.

**Susan**   I'm ... sorry.

**Symes**   Continue, Mr Langdon.

**Eric**   Well, Susan brought the glasses to the table and gave us each one.

**Symes**   Where did she put your father's?

**Eric**   On his right.

**Symes**   Neil's side?

**Eric**   Yes.

**Symes**   Go on.

**Eric**   Just after Susan sat down, the lights went out.

**Symes**   A power failure?

**Eric**   Yes. We were expecting it as it had been announced on the radio. There were candles on the table ready.

**Symes**   What time was this?

**Eric**   Eight o'clock.

**Symes**   Had anyone touched their wine before the lights went out?

**Eric**   No, there wasn't time.

**Symes**   What happened then?

**Eric**   After a few moments Neil lit the candles. Father suggested a toast to the new will and we all drank.

**Symes**   Everyone?

**Eric**   Yes. Father remarked that his wine tasted rather odd. Then he suddenly ... choked and fell back in his chair gasping for breath.

**Symes**   Did he let go of the wine glass?

**Eric**  I'm almost sure he didn't because Susan tried to take it from him.

**Symes**  What did you do?

**Eric**  It was obvious that father was very sick. We had to help him — I got his shirt open and Neil brought him a drink of water, but it didn't help. His gasps grew more violent and I rang the doctor — the phone was in the next room. He . . . died a few minutes later.

**Symes**  Between that time and the time the doctor arrived, did any of you move anything in the room — the wine, for example?

**Eric**  No. We just sat and waited.

**Symes**  One last question, Mr Langdon — do you believe your father was murdered?

**Eric**  Yes.

**Symes**  Did *you* murder your father?

**Eric**  No!

**Symes**  Thank you.

**Coroner**  Mr Langdon, did the wine taste odd to you?

**Eric**  I . . . can't remember.

**Coroner**  Did you hate your father?

**Eric**  No. I disliked him because he tried to rule my life — but not enough to kill him.

**Coroner**  Thank you. You may step down.

(**Eric** *returns to his seat.*)

**Symes**  I call Susan Langdon.

(**Susan** *rises and goes to the witness-box.*)

**Announcer**  Susan Langdon is twenty-eight and unmarried. She is a fairly successful artist.

**Symes**  Miss Langdon, do you agree with your brother's evidence? Is that the way it happened?

**Susan**  Yes, I think so.

**Symes**  Why did you come home on the day of your father's death?

**Susan**  Eric told you — to try to change his mind about the will.

**Symes**  Did you think the new will unfair?

**Susan**  Of course.

**Symes**  Where did you go for your drive during the afternoon?

**Susan**  Into Casewell to call on friends.

**Symes**  Did you visit any shops?

**Susan**  Yes, I went to a department store to buy cigarettes.

**Symes**  Does that store sell pesticides — like rat poison?

**Coroner**  Mr Symes — really!

**Symes**  I withdraw the question. Miss Langdon, at dinner that night,
did you drink some of the wine before your father collapsed?

**Susan**   Yes.

**Symes**   Did it taste odd?

**Susan**   It did rather. I thought it was just cheap wine.

**Symes**   Did you add anything to the wine as you were pouring it?

**Susan**   Of course not.

**Symes**   Or to your father's wine?

**Susan**   No!

**Symes**   Why did you try to take your father's glass from him after he collapsed?

**Susan**   I thought he might smash it and hurt himself.

**Symes**   Did any of you move anything in the room after he collapsed?

**Susan**   No.

**Symes**   Miss Langdon, did you murder your father?

**Susan**   The thought never entered my head.

**Symes**   Thank you, Miss Langdon.

**Coroner**   Miss Langdon, did you hate your father?

**Susan**   He wasn't worthy of hate. I just didn't bother with him.

**Coroner**   Why?

**Susan**   He believed my painting was a waste of time. Even when I made a success of it, he couldn't bring himself to admit he was wrong.

**Coroner**   Thank you. You may step down.

(**Susan** *returns to her seat.*)

**Symes**   I call Neil Langdon.

(**Neil** *rises and goes to the witness-box.*)

**Announcer**   Neil Langdon, the youngest of the children, is twenty-one and a student.

**Symes**  Mr Langdon, you are a student?

**Neil**  Yes.

**Symes**  Who supports you?

**Neil**  I support myself. I work in a factory at weekends.

**Symes**  Did your father refuse to help you — with money?

**Neil**  Yes. He wanted me to go into the family business, especially after Eric had left home. When I refused, he kicked me out.

**Symes**  And you hated him for this?

**Neil**  No — but I didn't miss him much either.

**Symes**  Did you consider the new will unfair?

**Neil**  It was more unfair to Eric and Susan than to me. They had to put up with him much longer.

**Symes**  I see. Do you agree with the evidence given by your brother and sister?

**Neil**  I do. They had no reason to lie.

**Symes**  Mr Langdon, one of you must be lying.

**Neil**  Not if father committed suicide.

**Symes**  Do you believe he *did* commit suicide?

**Neil**  It's the only reasonable explanation, isn't it?

**Symes**  That I doubt, Mr Langdon. What did you do during the afternoon while your father rested?

**Neil**  I read a book.

**Symes**  That night during dinner, your father's wine glass was placed on his right, near you.

**Neil**  I suppose so.

**Symes**  It was you who lit the candles?

**Neil**  Yes.

**Symes**  How long after the lights went out did you do this?

**Neil**  About thirty seconds.

**Symes**  Why the delay?

**Neil**  My eyes weren't accustomed to the dark. I couldn't find the matches.

**Symes**  Could you see your father's wine glass in the darkness?

**Neil**  I couldn't see anything.

**Symes**  It was right next to you. Can you remember if the curtains on the window were closed or open?

**Neil**  Open, I think.

**Symes**  So some light would have entered the room?

**Neil**  I suppose so.

**Symes**  Did the wine taste odd to you?

**Neil**  No. But I don't know much about wines.

**Symes**   Mr Langdon, did you murder your father?

**Neil**   No!

**Symes**   Thank you.

**Coroner**   Mr Langdon, do you miss your father now?

**Neil**   No.

**Coroner**   You may step down.

(**Neil** *returns to his seat.*)

**Symes**   I call the police surgeon, Dr Richard Edgar.

(**Edgar** *rises and goes to the witness-box.*)

**Announcer**   Dr Edgar, in his official capacity, carried out an examination later that night.

**Symes**   Dr Edgar, what was the cause of Henry Langdon's death?

**Edgar**   Heart failure brought on by a massive dose of arsenic.

**Symes**   How long would it take such a dose to act?

**Edgar**   Only a few minutes. The victim would become violently ill and go into a coma.

**Symes**   Could this dose be put in a glass of wine without the victim detecting it?

**Edgar**   It's possible — if the wine was strong enough to disguise the taste.

**Symes**   Did you order an analysis of the wine used that night?

**Edgar**   I did.

**Symes**   What was the result?

**Edgar**   There was no arsenic in any of the wine.

**Symes**   And Henry Langdon's glass?

**Edgar**   A thorough analysis of the dregs of wine in the glass was made. There was not a trace of arsenic.

**Symes**   Could the glass have been wiped clean?

**Edgar**  No. More wine would have had to be put in because some dregs remained. Nor could it have been possible to switch glasses. In his first spasm Henry Langdon gripped his glass with a great deal of strength. We can therefore conclude, Mr Symes, that there was never arsenic in the wine Henry Langdon drank.

**Symes**  Could the arsenic have been in the dinner food?

**Edgar**  No. Mr Langdon would not have been alive to drink any wine.

**Symes**  Doctor, was there any other substance in the wine that did not belong there?

**Edgar**  Yes — essence of vanilla.

(**Dr Harris** *suddenly stands up.*)

**Harris**  Mr Coroner!

**Coroner**  Yes, Dr Harris?

**Harris**  May I add to Dr Edgar's evidence?

**Coroner**   Of course. You may speak from there.

**Harris**   Henry Langdon had a very strong allergy. He reacted violently to certain foods. Vanilla essence was one of them.

**Coroner**   Dr Edgar, was the vanilla in all of the wine or just Henry Langdon's glass?

**Edgar**   All of the wine.

**Coroner**   Dr Harris, what would be his reaction to this substance?

**Harris**   Quite a violent and immediate one. He would probably have difficulty in breathing — even choke.

**Coroner**   Could it kill him by inducing a heart attack?

**Harris**   Definitely not.

**Coroner**   Did his children know of this allergy?

**Harris**   They must have.

**Coroner**   Doctor Harris, you know the Langdon household fairly well. Is that so?

**Harris**   Yes.

**Coroner**   Where did Mr Langdon usually keep the wine?

**Harris**   On the sideboard.

**Coroner**   So anyone could have tampered with it during the afternoon?

**Harris**   It would have been easy.

**Coroner**   Thank you. Dr Edgar, you may step down.

(**Edgar** *returns to his seat.*)

Mr Symes, do you have any more witnesses?

**Symes**   No, Mr Coroner.

**Coroner**   Then I will retire to consider my findings. Mr Symes, if you will accompany me.

(*The* **Coroner** *and* **Symes** *leave.*)

**Announcer**   Well, there you have it. Who killed Sir Henry Langdon and how was it done? Somewhere in all that evidence is a clue that will lead to a murderer. Remember that it is proof we need — guesswork is simply not enough. So would you, the 'jury', now consider your findings. Weigh the facts carefully, go over them, discuss them, think about them. It's in there somewhere, I'm sure it is!

*CURTAIN*

## Who Did It?

Now that *A Taste of Wine* has been performed, it's time for the audience to find out who actually *was* responsible for the murder of Sir Henry Langdon. One good way of having fun and discovering the murderer is to have the cast remain on the stage for close questioning by the audience.

Members of the audience, using the events described in the play, take it in turn to fire questions at particular characters. The characters must reply using only information from the play. It won't take long for the audience to discover the murderer.